THE DYSPRAXIC LEARNER

of related interest

Understanding Dyspraxia
A Guide for Parents and Teachers
Maureen Boon
ISBN 978 1 84905 069 2
eISBN 978 0 85700 259 4

Can I tell you about Dyspraxia?
A guide for friends, family and professionals
Maureen Boon
Illustrated by Imogen Hallam
ISBN 978 1 84905 447 8
eISBN 978 0 85700 824 4

Can't Play Won't Play
Simply Sizzling Ideas to get the
Ball Rolling for Children with Dyspraxia
Sharon Drew and Elizabeth Atter
ISBN 978 1 84310 601 2
eISBN 978 1 84642 758 9

Beating Dyspraxia with a Hop, Skip and a Jump
A Simple Exercise Program to Improve Motor Skills
at Home and School, Revised Edition
Geoff Platt
ISBN 978 1 84905 560 4
eISBN 978 0 85700 948 7

THE DYSPRAXIC LEARNER
STRATEGIES FOR SUCCESS

ALISON PATRICK

Jessica Kingsley *Publishers*
London and Philadelphia

First published in 2015
by Jessica Kingsley Publishers
73 Collier Street
London N1 9BE, UK
and
400 Market Street, Suite 400
Philadelphia, PA 19106, USA

www.jkp.com

Library of Congress Cataloging in Publication Data
Patrick, Alison, 1964-
 The dyspraxic learner : strategies for success / Alison Patrick.
   pages cm
 Includes bibliographical references.
 ISBN 978-1-84905-594-9 (alk. paper)
 1. Children with disabilities--Education. 2. Movement disorders in children. 3.
Apraxia. I. Title.
 LC4015.P325 2015
 371.9--dc23

                        2014036670

British Library Cataloguing in Publication Data
A CIP catalogue record for this book is available from the British Library

ISBN 978 1 84905 594 9
eISBN 978 1 78450 049 8

Printed and bound in Great Britain

MIX
Paper from
responsible sources
FSC
www.fsc.org   FSC® C013056

To my family

ACKNOWLEDGEMENTS

With thanks to:

Various librarians: Rebecca Evans at UCA, Sharon Swithinbank at Hampshire Library Service, and Claire Nicholas-Walker at the British Library, for either obtaining texts and articles or for doing some research to help me with text sources.

Lucy Alexander and Francis Maunze of the Royal College of Psychiatrists for their help when I was seeking to use an A.J. Annell text from the 1940s.

Barbara Houseman, voice coach and acting director, for her very helpful advice on deep breathing and 'Cameras out' techniques.

My student services and library colleagues from UCA, whose collaboration and support I greatly appreciate.

All the students with SpLDs I have ever taught or worked with.

Rachel Menzies, Sarah Hamlin, Kate Mason and Robert Rorison of Jessica Kingsley Publishers for their support and advice.

My father and mother, Alec and Anne Ellis, for their advice and encouragement during the writing process.

Finally, thank you to my long-suffering children, Matthew, William and Harriet, for their encouragement and support while I was writing this book. And thank you to my husband, Roger, for his wholehearted support at a time when he was busy with other projects.

CONTENTS

INTRODUCTION

Of all the key specific learning differences (SpLD) (autism, Asperger syndrome, dyslexia and dyspraxia), dyspraxia possesses the most interesting 'melting pot' mix of physical and mental characteristics. *The Dyspraxic Learner* is written for secondary school, college or university teachers who want to know more about dyspraxia, how it affects their students and the support strategies that can be used to create a successful learning environment for learners with dyspraxia. This book also aims to be of value to learners with dyspraxia themselves (or their friends and relatives), who are seeking an understanding of dyspraxia and supportive strategies. The dyspraxic mind and physical dyspraxia are looked at in depth, partly to foster greater understanding of dyspraxia but also to offer strategies for physical and psychological support.

Dyslexia is the predominant SpLD, with the strongest research base and the broadest media coverage. Dyspraxic (and dyslexic) students often do not know very much about the strengths their SpLD brings, or about alleviating strategies for the weaknesses. Statistically, at any time, teachers probably have at least one learner with dyspraxic tendencies in their classroom. Currently, due to the complex nature of dyspraxia, professionals can often be aware of some aspects of this SpLD, while remaining oblivious to other factors. Unfortunately, dyspraxia is too often associated with its most negative connotation, clumsiness. Ultimately, I believe that informed teachers can empower their dyspraxic students and that an increased understanding of dyspraxia can enhance a student's development potential.

This book aims to look at all manifestations of dyspraxia, all of which will impact in different ways on a student's life:

- Motor coordination
  - pen grip
  - handwriting
  - poor PE skills, e.g. catching, throwing, running.

- Muscle tone/joints
  - handwriting
  - poor PE skills
  - lethargy.
- Posture
  - slouching at desk
  - concentration affected.
- Balance
  - poor PE skills.
- Spatial awareness
  - accident prone.
- Visual and auditory processing
  - reading and writing difficulties.
- Planning and organisation
  - classroom and study skills.
- Attention deficits
  - inattentiveness in the classroom
  - daydreaming
  - inconsistent performance.
- Memory deficits
  - difficulties absorbing and processing information learned
  - inconsistent performance.
- Sleeplessness
  - fatigue.

All of the above can have emotional consequences for the learner with dyspraxia, and can affect life generally through:

- low self-esteem
- difficulties with social interaction
- stress and anxiety.

The variety of ways in which dyspraxia can manifest in the classroom shows the potential for educational disruption for the dyspraxic, in secondary and tertiary education. Although the difficulties of dyspraxia can, potentially, have a negative impact on educational attainment, some of these difficulties can be lessened, as long as the strengths which dyspraxia brings are nurtured in an academic context.

Obviously, by the secondary stage of education, a number of individual subjects will be studied and some difficulties will be specific to particular subjects. For example, science and food or design technology can bring practical considerations for the dyspraxic. This book does not discuss difficulties that might occur in individual subjects, but focuses on dyspraxic literacy difficulties, because difficulties with literacy affect most aspects of learning.

It should be emphasised that this book is researched and written from a teacher's perspective, rather than a medical perspective. Because of the diverse, pervasive nature of dyspraxia, this is a book of contrasting parts, a mixture of theory and practice. The first chapter focuses on defining dyspraxia and examining dyspraxic strengths and weaknesses. Chapter Two focuses on the diverse array of factors affecting physical dyspraxia, and offers supportive strategies. Chapters Three and Four are more practical, focusing on dyspraxia in an educational context. Chapter Three discusses literacy difficulties in the context of dyspraxia, and includes strategies for reading and writing. Chapter Four contains study skills strategies to bolster independent learning and to enhance performance. Chapter Five focuses on the neurological consequences of dyspraxia for the mind, focusing on memory, sleep and obsessive thoughts. Chapter Six focuses on the emotional consequences of dyspraxia, with strategies for coping with emotional volatility, low self-esteem, anxiety and stress. Strategies for social skills are also detailed. The final chapter focuses on dyspraxia in the workplace.

There is a caveat to all the strategies and methods listed in this book. Dyspraxia is on a spectrum, so some learners will be more severely affected than others and dyspraxic individuals will tend to have a 'cocktail' of symptoms rather than the whole gamut of attributes. Each learner with dyspraxia is unique and effective strategies will vary between individuals. This has already been evidenced through research undertaken by dyspraxia expert Professor Amanda Kirby, which demonstrated that 31 children with developmental coordination disorder (DCD) all had a different symptom profile (Kirby 2004, cited in Kirby, Davies and Bryant 2005, p.123). For this reason no individual strategy in this book will work for all learners, and strategies will need to be tested, tried and tailored to suit individual needs.

CHAPTER ONE
UNDERSTANDING DYSPRAXIA

Dyspraxia is broad in its manifestation, affecting both the body and the mind and having comorbidity not only with dyslexia but with other specific learning differences (SpLD) such as Asperger syndrome and attention deficit disorder as well.

Definitions

The word 'dyspraxia' comes from two Greek words, 'dys' and 'praxis'. Praxis is the Greek word for action or practice: 'The ability to interact successfully with the physical environment; to ideate, plan, organize, and carry out a sequence of unfamiliar actions; and to do what one needs and wants to do' (Stock Kranowitz 2005, p.316). 'Dys' is the Greek prefix 'bad'. When translated literally, dyspraxia means 'bad practice'.

The modern term dyspraxia seems to have its origins in a neurological context, where the term 'apraxia' represented an acquired disorder, and 'dys' was then used to represent a developmental disorder: dyspraxia (Steinman, Mostofsky and Denckla 2010, p.73). The Dyspraxia Foundation defines dyspraxia as 'an impairment or immaturity of the organisation of movement. It is associated with problems of perception, language and thought' (Dyspraxia Foundation 2014a). The Leeds Consensus Statement gives a good basic diagnostic definition of developmental coordination disorder which can be used to define the motor aspects of dyspraxia as well:

> The marked impairment has a significant, negative impact on activities of daily living – such as dressing, feeding, riding a bicycle – and/or on academic achievement such as through poor handwriting skills. Core aspects of the disorder include difficulties with gross and/or fine motor skills, which may be apparent in locomotion, agility, manual dexterity,

complex skills (e.g. ball games) and/or balance. (Economic and Social Research Council 2006, p.3)

There have been numerous definitions for dyspraxia historically but, nevertheless, dyspraxia remains subject to misinterpretation. Traditionally, children with dyspraxia have been described as 'clumsy' children, not a term that recognises the singular abilities of the dyspraxic mindset. Neurologist Dr Sasson S. Gubbay conceived the term 'Clumsy Child Syndrome' in his 1975 book, *The Clumsy Child* (Sutton Hamilton 2002, p.1435). Certainly there have been 'clumsy' individuals in all societies throughout history and they existed a long time before the terms 'dyspraxia' or 'developmental coordination disorder' were coined. Helen Burns, Jane Eyre's school friend in the famous Charlotte Brontë novel of 1847, is reputed to have been the first dyspraxic character in English literature:

> Then learn from me, not to judge by appearances: I am, as Miss Scatcherd said, slatternly; I seldom put, and never keep, things in order; I am careless; I forget rules; I read when I should learn my lessons; I have no method; and sometimes I say, like you, I cannot *bear* to be subjected to systematic arrangements. (Brontë 1953 (original v.1847), p.74)

In the 1940s and 1950s, Professor of Psychiatry A.L. Annell described children who move awkwardly, are 'poor' at games, 'hopeless' at gymnastics, write badly and cannot concentrate. They cannot sit still, tie shoelaces or fasten buttons properly, may bump into objects, break glass, slide off their chairs, kick their desks and may even read badly. Annell notes that performance may be worse when the child is anxious or self-conscious (Annell, cited in the *British Medical Journal* 1962, p.1665). This really demonstrates that dyspraxia has been noticed in the classroom for many years; and the attributes associated with it are not just a modern phenomenon.

Dyspraxia or Developmental Coordination Disorder (DCD)?

There is an element of confusion about dyspraxia and developmental coordination disorder. In Britain both terms are used, often interchangeably, and there can be some confusion among practitioners about whether DCD and dyspraxia are the same condition. In their article on the 'enigma' of dyspraxia and DCD, John Gibbs, Jeanette and Richard Appleton argue that different professionals have had an impact on how coordination difficulties are defined and this has resulted in different terminologies (Gibbs *et al.* 2007).

Although there are similarities, dyspraxia differs from DCD because its definition encompasses perceptual and thinking differences. The Dyspraxia Foundation describes dyspraxia as:

> A form of developmental coordination disorder... While DCD is often regarded as an umbrella term to cover motor coordination difficulties, dyspraxia refers to those people who have additional problems planning, organising and carrying out movements in the right order in everyday situations. Dyspraxia can also affect articulation and speech, perception and thought. (Dyspraxia Foundation 2013a)

The significant role that the mind plays in this condition cannot be underestimated. This book is by definition about dyspraxia because one of the key focuses is the dyspraxic mind and its impact on learning. I would be reluctant to lose the term dyspraxia because it is well established in many people's minds and, of course, has linguistic associations with another key SpLD, dyslexia.

Causes

The Dyspraxia Foundation explains that, for most dyspraxics, there is no 'clinical neurological abnormality'. But research has found that it may be related to the central nervous system and immaturities in neurone development (Dyspraxia Foundation 2014b). An immaturity in the development of neural pathways could be seen to result in physical and cognitive difficulties. There could, for example, be an impact on teenage and adult thinking patterns, resulting in repetitive or even obsessive thoughts.

Hereditary

Students with SpLDs often have parents, relatives and siblings with similar traits. Forty years ago assessment for dyslexia and dyspraxia was not nearly so prevalent. In the last 20 years, research has advanced rapidly, particularly research into dyslexia. Recognition of dyspraxia will improve because diagnosis is already in place for a current generation of students.

Comorbidity and heredity could have interesting implications where, for example, a child growing up with the challenges that dyspraxia brings, is growing up in a home environment where a parent is, for example, on the autistic spectrum and is facing their own challenges.

Birth

Research tends to show that DCD is more likely in premature and low birth weight children (Holsti, Grunau and Whitfield 2002, Edwards *et al.* 2011 and Zwicker *et al.* 2013). Chartered psychologist David Grant has found that, 'In my experience, and that of others [e.g. see Gubbay 1985, cited in Drew 2005], birth complications are reported in about 50% of dyspraxics' (Grant n.d., p.9).

Diagnosis

It is thought that dyspraxia affects between six and ten per cent of the population, leading to the likelihood that there is at least one learner with dyspraxia in every classroom. Classroom, seminar and lecture theatre adjustments are particularly important for the six to ten per cent of pupils who have dyspraxic tendencies because some of these students will never be assessed for dyspraxia.

The complexity of dyspraxia with its framework of mental, cognitive and physical issues can easily lead to confusion about how to treat or to assess dyspraxia. Physiotherapist Pam Versfeld argues that:

> There are no formal criteria for a diagnosis of dyspraxia. This makes it very confusing: different people use the term dyspraxia in different ways... Including all these different developmental difficulties into one diagnosis has its drawbacks because it prevents clear thinking about the different factors contributing [to] the everyday difficulties the child is experiencing. (Versfeld 2007)

Dyspraxia is a condition with a medical and an educational impact. As a result of its physical and mental nature, there are various routes for assessment of dyspraxia. GPs will either direct their patients to an occupational therapist (OT) who can only focus on physical dyspraxia, or to a psychologist, who can look at cognitive aspects of dyspraxia. They might also refer to a neurologist for diagnosis, which is followed up with OT support. This can cause diagnostic confusion. The specialist teacher assessor can also assess for dyspraxia in an educational context (SpLD Assessment Standards Committee 2013, pp.1–2).

Chartered psychologist David Grant believes that identification of an SpLD is 'a clinical judgement...in which labels are best viewed as having fuzzy edges rather than box-type characteristics' (Grant n.d., p.2) and he has encountered diagnoses where although an SpLD has been identified, a co-existing SpLD has been overlooked (Grant n.d., p.7). 'Although books about dyspraxia suggest there is a classic profile, in practice I find that there are many variations' (Grant n.d., p.10).

Over-zealous labelling

People still mistakenly believe that if a child is simply clumsy or has illegible handwriting, then they must be dyspraxic. In their article entitled 'Dyspraxia or developmental coordination disorder? Unravelling the enigma', John Gibbs *et al.* discuss the increasing tendency to label awkward or clumsy children as dyspraxic (Gibbs *et al.* 2007). Of course, this is why it is so important for different practitioners involved with teenagers and adults with SpLD to be aware of all facets of dyspraxia. Children and teenagers are generally at a stage of their development where they can at times be clumsy, forgetful or disorganised. This does not mean that they are dyspraxic.

Leading authority on autism Professor Simon Baron-Cohen believes that everyone falls on a continuum of autistic traits and that the diagnosis should be influenced by environment as well as assessment score. Individuals who are coping with their autism may not require a diagnosis because they do not need intervention (Dommett 2011, p.30). This is applicable to dyspraxia, with its broad spectrum too: without a need for intervention, there is no need for diagnosis. However, assessment for dyspraxia can be important in an educational and a medical context. In an educational setting, it can be important because it can result in, for example, extra time and a laptop for exams. These exam concessions become increasingly vital for teenage dyspraxics tackling GCSEs, A-levels and degree level exams, ensuring parity with other students. At tertiary level, educational intervention can also facilitate access to specialist teacher support or mentoring, both of which can be an invaluable resource for the student with dyspraxia. Assessment for dyspraxia will also be important where physical or mental difficulties require medical intervention.

Treatment

I have worked with students with dyspraxia who have been well served physically by occupational therapy in early childhood. I have also worked with students who have excellent mental strategies from educational psychologists. Those psychological strategies are particularly advantageous for teenage and adult dyspraxics. As a result of its diverse nature there are many other interventions available for dyspraxia, some of which are available from qualified practitioners, others being lifestyle choices:

- Alexander Technique
- physiotherapy
- podiatrist
- speech therapist
- Cognitive behavioural therapy
- counselling
- gym
- mindfulness
- yoga.

This book will discuss these strategies in more detail.

Unfortunately, there are many individuals who grow up feeling debilitated by their awkwardness and difference, and are very poorly supported for coping with their dyspraxia. They have never realised that there is a significant reason for their physical difficulties or the emotional challenges they face. For those pupils with dyspraxic tendencies, who may never go down the medical assessment route, the best accommodations in a classroom are achieved through being aware of:

- physical difficulties and strategies to compensate
- different styles of learning.

Comorbidity

There can be comorbidity between these key SpLDs:

- dyslexia
- dyspraxia/DCD
- autism spectrum disorders (ASD) (including Asperger syndrome)
- AD(H)D.

That is, two or more can occur in an individual at the same time.

The Make-up of Neuro-Diversity

This is a document for discussion. Concentrating mainly on the difficulties of those with neuro-diversity. It must, however, be pointed out that many people with neuro-diversity are excellent at maths, coordination, reading etc. We are people of extremes.

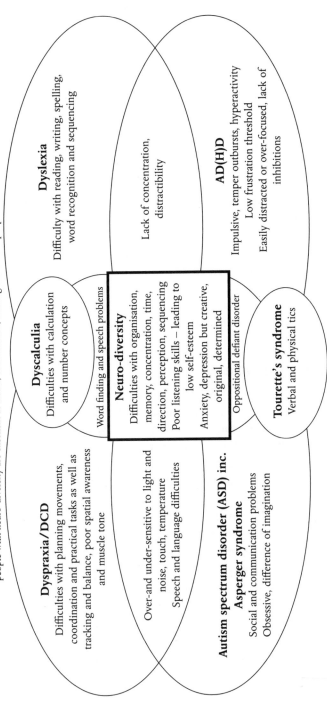

Dyslexia
Difficulty with reading, writing, spelling, word recognition and sequencing

Lack of concentration, distractibility

AD(H)D
Impulsive, temper outbursts, hyperactivity
Low frustration threshold
Easily distracted or over-focused, lack of inhibitions

Dyscalculia
Difficulties with calculation and number concepts

Word finding and speech problems

Neuro-diversity
Difficulties with organisation, memory, concentration, time, direction, perception, sequencing
Poor listening skills – leading to low self-esteem
Anxiety, depression but creative, original, determined

Oppositional defiant disorder

Tourette's syndrome
Verbal and physical tics

Dyspraxia/DCD
Difficulties with planning movements, coordination and practical tasks as well as tracking and balance, poor spatial awareness and muscle tone

Over-and under-sensitive to light and noise, touch, temperature
Speech and language difficulties

Autism spectrum disorder (ASD) inc. Asperger syndrome
Social and communication problems
Obsessive, difference of imagination

Figure 1.1 Diagram depicting the make-up of neuro-diversity
(Colley 2006, p.161)

Figure 1.1, 'The make-up of neuro-diversity' (Colley 2006, p.161), provides an excellent visual aid to show the convergences and divergences between SpLDs. This tool has been invaluable to me when working with students with different SpLDs. This comorbidity between different SpLDs means that dyspraxics can also have other SpLDs. Autism and Asperger syndrome are autism spectrum disorders (ASD); dyspraxia is not. However, dyspraxia does share characteristics with ASDs, particularly Asperger syndrome.

This comorbidity can, unfortunately, cause diagnostic confusion with different SpLDs sharing similar traits. It could be argued that currently there is an element of over-labelling, with some students seeing a variety of professionals, the result being that they are labelled with all the broad category SpLDs, because they all share common characteristics. It can be really helpful for specialist teacher assessors to identify dyspraxic tendencies because the needs of learners with dyspraxia diverge from the needs of their dyslexic peers. Ultimately, psychiatric definitions and professional judgements discriminating between diagnostic differences have to be deferred to and the most important outcome is that the most needy learners have been assessed and qualify for support.

Asperger syndrome

There seems to be a clear relationship between dyspraxia and ASDs, even although dyspraxia is not on the autism spectrum. In my own experience, when working with students with Asperger syndrome, it is as if I am looking at some of the traits of dyspraxia through a microscope to find them magnified. For example, any issues the dyspraxic might have with obsessiveness about small details or daily routines seem to be exacerbated in Asperger syndrome.

The National Autistic Society recognises that for autism spectrum disorders, 'some of the characteristics of the two conditions overlap, meaning that both have many similar characteristics' (The National Autistic Society 2014). The National Autistic Society draws a distinction between the causes of poor social skills experienced by people with dyspraxia and a key characteristic of Asperger syndrome, 'impairment in social intelligence'. Social difficulties experienced by the dyspraxic are not fundamental to the condition but are an outcome of physical difficulties leading to isolation (The National Autistic Society 2014). A key trait of people with dyspraxia is empathy, whereas for people with Asperger syndrome, cognitive empathy can be impaired (Baron-Cohen *et al.* 2014). So, although there are similarities between dyspraxia and ASD, there are key differences too.

Motor difficulties seem to present in Asperger syndrome as well as in dyspraxia. Clinical psychologist Tony Attwood devotes a chapter of his book, *The Complete Guide to Asperger's Syndrome* (2008), to movement and coordination. According to McCleery *et al.*, difficulties with motor skills seem to be a common experience of autism and this can have an impact on social and language skills (McCleery *et al.* 2013). Research by Dzuik *et al.* into motor skills deficits in autistic children suggested that dyspraxia could be a fundamental feature of autism (Dzuik *et al.* 2007, p.738). This overlap between dyspraxia and autism means that 'it is important that the person making the diagnosis has the relevant experience and knowledge to make a thorough assessment (National Autistic Society 2014).

Dyslexia

Links can be seen between dyspraxia and dyslexia as well. Comorbidity occurs with organisational and literacy difficulties. Dyspraxic people can be dyslexic, but dyspraxics can have literacy difficulties without being dyslexic. Dyspraxics and dyslexics also seem to share a short-term memory deficit. In fact, I have never worked with these two SpLDs without encountering short-term memory difficulties.

Attention deficit disorder (ADD)

There is some comorbidity between dyspraxia and ADD because both SpLDs display difficulties with:

- distractibility
- concentration
- listening and following instructions
- organisation.

However, the comorbidity is limited to these areas, and learners with ADD do not seem to exhibit the physical difficulties or many of the other cognitive strengths and weaknesses which are associated with dyspraxia.

Brain dominance

Although left and right brain hemispheres are responsible for different cognitive functions, the left and right brains in dyspraxics (and dyslexics) seem to be wired unusually. According to author Thomas West, the neurologist Dr Norman Geschwind found that some individuals have relatively 'symmetrical brains' and that this symmetry can lead not only to 'special abilities' but to 'special areas of difficulty' as well (West 1991, p.13). West argues that, for some, the roles assigned to the two different hemispheres can be reversed, and for others, language abilities can be found on both sides (West 1991, p.14).

According to the Dyspraxia Foundation, for dyspraxic individuals, both brain hemispheres do not seem to respond in a coordinated way. There may be no marked handedness preference and this will impact on handwriting skills (Dyspraxia Foundation 2014c). This can result in learners with dyspraxia displaying different handedness for different tasks. For example, cutlery might be held in a left-handed way while scissors are held in the right hand. When pre-school children are first holding a pencil to learn to write, the child with dyspraxia might show no marked preference for left- or right-handed grip. Neurologist Martha Denckla refers to a paradox where the 'good' hand may not perform as well as the hand that is not used (Denckla 1984, p.251). This indecisiveness between the two brain hemispheres could well be one of the factors that causes handwriting difficulties for dyspraxics throughout their lives.

Various researchers have found left-handedness to be statistically more prevalent in individuals with DCD or dyspraxia than it would be in the general population. Certainly, when teaching students with SpLDs, I teach quite a large number of left-handers. There is a common assumption that left-handedness means that a person is right-brain dominant (Broca's Rule) and that left-handed dyspraxics, as a result of this, must be creative and less language oriented. It is not as straightforward as this and writing hand does not necessarily seem to be an indicator of brain dominance. Dr M.K. Holder of the Handedness Institute at Indiana University refers, in his Public Interest Survey, to left-handed surgeons and dentists operating right-handed (Holder 2005a). It can be interesting to observe brain dominance in learners by watching the following:

- thumb on top when hands and thumbs crossed
- leg or arm on top when arms or legs crossed
- foot used to kick a ball
- hand used to catch a ball.

The dominant foot for kicking a ball might be the right foot, even though a person is left-handed. There does not seem to be anything as straightforward as a crossover between the brain with the right-hand, more creative side of the brain being dominant for left-handers and the left-hand, more logical brain being dominant for right-handers. Holder notes that 'a majority of left-handers also seem to have a left-hemispheric brain specialization for language abilities' (Holder 2005b).

The power of dyspraxia

If society had not needed its 'clumsy' individuals, would they have survived? On a simplistic view at least, Darwin's theory of 'survival of the fittest' would seem to suggest that if there were anything inherently weak about dyspraxia, then dyspraxics would not have evolved beyond the world of primitive man. Might an ancient tribe have valued a dyspraxic's differences, even if they were useless at hunting, tracking a beast with even a semblance of quietness, or sewing a loincloth for the winter months? Some of the differences associated with dyspraxia certainly seem to be beneficial. Whether they compensate for the weaknesses is a moot point and depends on how and in what circumstances they manifest themselves and how they are viewed by the individuals affected.

So, before engaging with the troubles which dyspraxia may cause, it is worth looking at the strengths which often seem to accompany it. One of the key features of dyspraxia is 'thinking differently'. When engaged in any conceptual task, the dyspraxic is likely to approach it from a different angle and this can lead to an inventive or creative perspective, to clever problem-solving and strategies, and to developments in thinking about particular areas.

Cognitive strengths

In a speech to the Orton Dyslexia Society, neurologist Norman Geschwind argued that the advantages of dyslexia might well outweigh the disadvantages, 'the important advantages conferred on those who carry the predisposition to these conditions may outweigh the obvious dramatic disadvantages' (Geschwind 1982, cited in West 1991, p.20). Similarly, there may be cognitive difficulties associated with dyspraxia, but there may also be cognitive strengths, many of which are shared with dyslexic thinkers too.

The physical attributes of dyspraxia may at times be demeaning, but the cognitive benefits of brains which are wired to think differently to the norm cannot be underestimated. In spite of tripping up, dressing haphazardly and failing to catch a ball, the dyspraxic has a potential advantage in the classroom and in the workplace because of a different cognitive style. This difference in mindset will always be apparent in group activities and team work.

In listing common dyspraxic strengths, it should be noted that these strengths are as variable and versatile as dyspraxia itself. Some dyspraxics have lifelong difficulties with literacy; others are highly literate, their literacy contrasting with that of their peers. Some dyspraxics struggle primarily with organisation and time management, while others are highly efficient at organising not only themselves, but other people as well. Strengths do not necessarily compensate for weaknesses and it is unlikely that a dyspraxic would have all the strengths or all the weaknesses associated with dyspraxia. There does seem to be a tendency, however, for the cognitive traits which are discussed in this chapter to prevail in dyspraxia.

Key strengths that are associated with dyspraxia include:

- verbal intelligence
- attention to detail
- creativity
- lateral thinking
- holistic thinking
- strategic thinking
- problem solving
- conceptual thinking
- inventiveness
- empathy
- determination
- motivation.

It really is worthwhile for learners with dyspraxia to be aware of these potential strengths, because often they have very clever thinking skills but are more aware of their negative academic and sporting experiences.

Verbal intelligence

People with dyspraxia can have a high verbal intelligence, an aptitude for language which can lead to a strong vocabulary. When assessed, they will often perform highly in verbal tasks. Gubbay noted that people with dyspraxia have a verbal intelligence that is significantly higher than performance IQ (Gubbay 1975, cited in Denckla 1984, p.246). As a result of this verbal intelligence, some dyspraxics are highly literate. Younger dyspraxics may take longer to read and write because of visual and auditory processing issues, but have literacy strengths as they get older because of an underlying verbal intelligence.

Attention to detail

Interestingly, according to Disability Salford, 'Many dyspraxic people and people with other non-verbal learning disabilities tend to focus on the incongruent details in a story rather than automatically form a coherent narrative. In general, this gives me a good eye for detail' (Disability Salford n.d.).

Creativity

According to the Dyspraxia Foundation, 'Many people with dyspraxia are very creative, determined, persistent and intelligent' (Dyspraxia Foundation 2014a). Certainly, this has been my experience of working with students who have SpLDs at a university which specialises solely in the arts.

Lateral thinking

The Civil Service Appraisal document, *The Dyslexia and Dyspraxia Toolkit: Enabling a Whole Organisation Approach*, acknowledges dyspraxic thinking skills when it instructs appraisers to 'Give credit for lateral thinking because dyslexia and dyspraxia are cognitive differences' (Todd 2011, p.31). Jacky Birnie of the University of Gloucestershire writes that, 'Asperger syndrome lateral thinking may come up with "right" answers which had not been anticipated by the tutor setting a standard essay exam.' (Birnie n.d., p.10) This could equally be applied to students with dyspraxia and could, in fact, affect exam results if marking structures are not expecting unusual (but accurate) answers.

Ross Cooper emphasises the importance of random association for lateral thinking and although his focus is dyslexia, this also has huge resonance for how learners with dyspraxia think, and demonstrates how easily the learner with dyspraxia can be underestimated in a traditional classroom environment:

But the importance to holistic thinking is extremely undervalued in the classroom. Random association is the underpinning of lateral thinking…Random association allows us to rethink what the organising principle of the information needs to be to suit the current purpose. (Cooper n.d., p.10)

Strategic thinking and problem solving

A key strength of dyspraxia is an ability to think strategically and to problem solve. Possibly these thinking skills have less opportunity to thrive during childhood education, but become more applicable at secondary school and beyond. 'The right-brained mode of thinking is ideally suited for problem solving, intuitive and holistic thinking, and quantum leaps in understanding: These are the very qualities that have aided humans to evolve into such technologically advanced beings' (University of Hull, n.d.(a) p.5).

Conceptual thinking

West recognises that people with SpLDs will often find supposedly easier concepts more difficult and more advanced ideas more straightforward to grasp (West 1991, p.69). This could be partly why some learners with dyspraxia find the simple building blocks of learning difficult to acquire but the more academic the context, the easier it becomes to engage and to apply the learning. This difference in thinking could also be an explanatory factor for difficulties students with dyspraxia have in concentrating and remaining attentive in the classroom.

Inventiveness

Inventiveness could well be a result of the attributes that are typically associated with strong dyspraxic thinking, where the lateral, problem-solving nature of the thinking often makes associations between ideas which might not instantly be connected or correlated, leading to inventive solutions.

Empathy

Teacher and author Geoff Brookes believes that the difficulties which accompany dyspraxia lead to an emotional perceptiveness and that this facet of the dyspraxic personality often leads them into caring professions

(*TES* 2003). Although a strength, this intuitive sensitivity towards others can have an extremely negative aspect for some dyspraxics, leading to hypersensitivity about the thoughts and motives of others and resulting in difficulties in establishing and maintaining sound social relationships.

Cognitive weaknesses

Cognitive weaknesses, some of which are interlinked, which will have an impact on learners with dyspraxia are:

- memory deficit
- planning and organisation
- concentration
- visual processing
- auditory processing
- sensory issues.

It is useful for students with dyspraxia to understand that, for example, not being able to recall what has been taught in a recent lesson or not being able to concentrate at all in the classroom, are deficits that relate to dyspraxia and these weaknesses do not mean that they are 'stupid'.

Memory deficit

Working and short-term memory are cognitive weaknesses for learners with dyspraxia. The Student Services department at the University of East London identifies the following difficulties which will occur for learners, as a result of memory deficits:

- forgetfulness
- recall of what has just been said
- remembering instructions
- information retrieval
- understanding group discussions
- mental arithmetic
- multi-tasking
- getting diverted
- time management and organisation.

(University of East London n.d.)

The Dyspraxia Group of New Zealand refer to the difficulty of gauging the progress or potential of learners with dyspraxia:

> Teachers may, find the child's ability to retain learning inconsistent... making it difficult to gauge either what the child's intellectual potential might be, or how much information the child has retained or can recall. He or she will certainly need to discover the child's strengths and encourage these in order to maintain self-esteem... Inconsistency means that a skill or ability today may be a disability tomorrow. This is not laziness – he simply can't (The Dyspraxia Support Group of New Zealand n.d.).

Ultimately, memory difficulties have the potential to have a detrimental impact on all aspects of dyspraxic learning.

Planning and organisation

Cognitive weaknesses in planning and motor planning difficulties are related, but weaknesses in planning and organisation could also result from memory difficulties (see Chapter Two). Cognitive difficulties with planning can lead to:

- indecisiveness
- impulsiveness
- difficulties structuring work
- time management difficulties
- untidiness
- multi-tasking difficulties.

For the learner with dyspraxia, 'Poor planning skills may mean that he needs constantly to know what is going to happen today, tonight, tomorrow, to plan ahead and repeat the plan often' (The Dyspraxia Support Group of New Zealand).

Concentration

Learners with dyspraxia may be easily distracted or even hyperactive in a learning setting. Work may at times be careless, with words crossed out as a result of inattentiveness:

> A perceived 'lack of concentration' may simply mean that his planning (or praxis) deserted him mid-task... These children need to learn, would

if they could, but – sometimes – can't… He or she is not dumb, not stupid, not lazy, and not often un-cooperative. (The Dyspraxia Support Group of New Zealand)

Research by Hanes and McCollum looks at links between the vestibular system and cognitive deficits such as poor concentration or weaknesses of short-term memory (Hanes and McCollum 2006, p.75). Difficulty in concentrating could also be attributed to the fact that learners with dyspraxia may think in a lateral and holistic manner.

Visual processing

As a result of weaknesses in visual processing, learners with dyspraxia may take longer to make sense of visual information. There may be difficulties in:

- visual discrimination
- visual sequencing
- visual memory.

All these visual difficulties can have an impact on reading and writing. According to the University of East London, this may also result in:

- disorientation
- slower reading examination questions
- slowness in learning to spatially navigate different environments.

'In combination with working memory, this weakness can affect automaticity; extra energy is required to concentrate on areas that are automatic for non-dyspraxic students' (University of East London n.d.).

Auditory processing

As a result of weaknesses in auditory processing, learners with dyspraxia may struggle with:

- auditory discrimination – resulting in difficulties with reading and writing
- auditory distractibility – making it more difficult to concentrate
- auditory memory – making it more difficult to retain what has been learned in the classroom

- auditory sequencing – making it more difficult to follow instructions.

Sensory issues

Some dyspraxics may be over- or under-sensitive to noise, light, taste, smell and touch. Tactile reactions, for example, can result in a refusal to wear certain fabrics, a dislike of physical contact or proximity, or an aversion to certain food consistencies and textures.

Splinter skills

It could be that learners with dyspraxia have what psychologists describe as 'splinter skills'. Perhaps some learners with dyspraxia might have a strength in one aspect of an area which is generally weak. For example, a poor speller might have a large, academic vocabulary which does not get used because of fears about spelling, or a learner with some visual processing difficulties might have excellent visual-spatial skills. A learner who is woeful at mathematics might be excellent at arithmetic.

If the needs of the learner with dyspraxia are ignored in the classroom or this type of learner is misunderstood, then they will flounder. But if accommodation is made for their difference in learning style, and strategies are applied to their difficulties, then they will often have the capability to flourish academically.

Famous dyspraxics

Unfortunately, although the internet attributes dyspraxia to several famous living people (including Stephen Fry and Bill Gates), I cannot find anything to substantiate these rumours, and these people are all of a generation when diagnosis of any SpLD was less prevalent. The following famous people have actually said they are dyspraxic and in each case the symptoms they mention would have had an impact in the classroom:

- Daniel Radcliffe says that he has mild dyspraxia, impacting on his handwriting, and tying shoelaces (*The Daily Telegraph* 2008b).

- In an interview with Francesca Ryan, Florence Welch of Florence and the Machine said that she had been dyslexic and dyspraxic and, therefore, was not really present mentally in the classroom (*The Daily Telegraph* 2009a). Interestingly, she was very creative and went on to art college.

- Max Kaufman (captain of the winning University Challenge team in 2008) was diagnosed with dyspraxia at an early age and is a resounding example of how clever and how literate dyspraxics can be, with a verbal IQ of 170 and a written IQ of 120 (*The Daily Telegraph* 2008a).

I am sceptical when I see dyspraxia attributed to historical figures, for example Sir Isaac Newton or Albert Einstein. Apparently, Albert Einstein walked around with his shoelaces untied. Does that necessarily indicate dyspraxia, or was it simply a man with his mind on other matters? It is necessary to remain grounded about the clever thinking patterns which accompany dyspraxia and other SpLDs and to remember that strategising and lateral thinking are not the sole preserve of dyspraxics or dyslexics. Non-dyspraxics can also possess these cognitive strengths. Neurologist Norman Geschwind noted that dyslexics can have non-dyslexic relatives who are left-handed and share the strengths of dyslexia without suffering from any of the weaknesses (Geschwind 1982, cited in West 1991, p.23).

CHAPTER TWO
PHYSICAL DYSPRAXIA

The interesting thing about dyspraxia, when compared with autism spectrum disorders (ASDs) or dyslexia, is the way in which dyspraxia can have such a pronounced effect, not only on the mind, but on physical skills as well. Current research suggests that dyspraxia results from underdeveloped neurons (nerve cell transmitters) preventing messages from passing efficiently between the brain and the body. This means that the neural pathways which would usually form to allow a task to be performed (even the most basic task of coordination, for example) are not formed properly. The more a task is performed efficiently the stronger the neural pathway will become, which is why practice and reinforcement of skills are particularly important for the learner with dyspraxia, for both physical and mental tasks. An example of current neural research giving dyspraxia a clearer definition is the work of Julie Werner, Sharon Cermak and Lisa Aziz-Zadeh, which links mirror neuron dysfunction with DCD (Werner *et al.* 2012).

For efficient neural messaging to occur a two-way transmission of messages is required, involving:

- sensory input
- motor output.

A dysfunction between sensory input and motor output seems to be central to physical dyspraxia.

(For a teacher's guide to the brain see the National Institute of Health and the National Institute of Neurological Disorders and Stroke 2005.)

Sensory input

Sensory input involves transmission of nerve impulses via neurons and is important for motor planning. Sensory integration of this input depends on various sensory systems:

- somatic (muscles and joints)
- visual
- auditory
- gustatory (taste)
- olfactory (smell)
- tactile (touch)
- vestibular system (body position, motion, balance, spatial awareness)
- proprioception (kinaesthetic) (body position, movement of body parts, coordination).

Motor output

Motor planning, a part of 'praxis', involves the planning and execution of a sequence of movements. (The other part of praxis is forming an idea of using a known movement to achieve a planned purpose.) Having received neural messages through sensory integration, the brain then transmits messages back to the muscles and joints. If the nerve impulses are compromised, as they seem to be in dyspraxia, this will have an effect on:

- joints and muscle tone
- coordination
- balance
- posture
- spatial awareness.

These physical components are not isolated and difficulties with one will often have an impact on another. Gubbay noted that for dyspraxics, some motor activities might actually be performed well, while others are performed badly (Gubbay 1975, cited in Denckla 1984, p.246). This can mean that fine motor skills are sound, while gross motor skills are weak or some fine or gross motor skills are sound while others are not. For example, difficulties with catching could be accompanied by proficiency in sewing. A very early indication of dyspraxia could be when a child never crawls but bottom shuffles instead. Occupational therapist Jill Christmas writes that in the opinion of many practitioners, crawling helps with fine motor skills, hand–eye coordination and posture and helps to integrate both sides of the body. (Christmas 2009). (See sections on *fine motor skills* and *gross motor skills* later in this chapter.)

Can I think of one good thing or key strength associated with the physical impact of dyspraxia? I cannot. Not one thing. People with dyslexia and dyspraxia often seem to be highly visual and creative but I have worked with students with dyspraxia who have struggled with finely coordinated creative skills such as drawing or sewing because of inherent weaknesses in their muscle tone and coordination. What sort of paradox is that for the dyspraxic? To be highly creative and yet unable to use all the physical tools available to them to realise their artistic creativity.

Vestibular skills

Weaknesses in neural transmission between the brain and the body have an impact on vestibular skills. Deficiencies in the functioning of the vestibular system, which is located in the inner ear, seem to have a significant impact on the physical symptoms of dyspraxia. Occupational therapist and educational psychologist Dr A.J. Ayres describes the vestibular system as 'the unifying system… All other types of sensation are processed in reference to this basic vestibular information' (Ayres 1979, cited in Stock Kranowitz 2005, p.115).

Vestibular relates to perception of body position (including the position of the head in relation to the body), balance, movement and spatial awareness. It also gives a sense of gravity, literally the position of the body in relation to the earth. The Vestibular Disorders Association describes the vestibular system as including, 'parts of the inner ear and brain that process the sensory information involved with controlling balance and eye movements' (Vestibular Disorders Association 2014a).

Proprioception is closely associated with the vestibular system, giving awareness of body position through vestibular and other sensory system input. Proprioception provides 'information about body position and movement of our body parts' (Stock Kranowitz 2005, p.54) and is 'the sensory information that we receive from our joints and muscles. This information is telling us about the position, movement, force, and direction needed for activities such as buttoning clothes, writing, screwing a lid on a jar' (Hopscotch Children's Therapy Centre 2012).

If all sensory information is processed in relation to the vestibular system, then it is not surprising that vestibular difficulties will have profound implications for the learner with dyspraxia, resulting in physical or cognitive effects on:

- visual and auditory perception
- spatial awareness
- balance and eye movements
- posture
- motion
- muscle maintenance
- coordination
- concentration.

All these skills will have an impact on planning and sequencing movements and on perceptual ability.

According to the Laboratory of Vestibular Neurophysiology at Johns Hopkins Hospital, although there is plenty of scientific knowledge about the vestibular part of the inner ear, 'key aspects of how the vestibular receptors perceive, process and report essential information are still mysterious' (Laboratory of Vestibular Neurophysiology n.d.). A fuller understanding of the causes of dyspraxia is very much dependent on continuing scientific research into the very complex area of the human brain.

Glue ear

The vestibular system is so near to the auditory system that if a child gets glue ear this can have an impact on balance and coordination. Hearing problems caused by glue ear might also affect literacy skills. Typically glue ear can begin to affect children at a critical stage when they are learning to read and write, thus affecting phonological awareness.

Muscles and joints

Children with dyspraxia can have muscle and joint problems affecting their physical movements, making dyspraxia a condition with very real physical difficulties. Muscle and joint weaknesses may be diagnosed as hypermobility and hypotonia:

- Joint hypermobility means that joints have a larger scope for movement than average. 'Double jointed' means hypermobile. Ballet dancers and circus performers are often hypermobile.
- Hypotonia is the medical term for poorly functioning muscle tone. Hypotonia often results in flat feet.

Loose joints and low muscle tone are key issues for many dyspraxics. However, a child who has hypotonia and hypermobility is not necessarily dyspraxic.

Although low muscle tone, a common feature of dyspraxia, manifests as a physical symptom, its origin is neurological, with inefficient messages from the brain regarding movement causing a weakness in the muscles. It is also worth noting that the vestibular system helps to maintain normal muscle tone, and weaknesses in the vestibular system will have an impact on muscles too. Low muscle tone has an impact on, for example, coordination and posture. Where muscle tone is low because of inefficient transmission of messages from the brain, muscles also become weakened over time because of these neural inefficiencies. This can have a resounding effect on day to day living and classroom performance for the student with dyspraxia from a very early age because it is quite simply exhausting to have a body which is physically inefficient. So, where a learner with dyspraxia might appear to tire easily or to be apathetic or lazy, this is not really the case at all, they are simply struggling with their physicality and allowances need to be made for this in a learning environment.

Muscle and joint effects

Low muscle tone can have an impact on both upper and lower limbs.

Upper limbs

A weakness in the wrist and forearm muscles can affect coordination, making it awkward to use any kind of tools – anything from a tin opener or scissors to a pair of garden shears or even a bow and arrow! In the classroom, pens and pencils will be held awkwardly and this will impact on quality and speed of handwriting. Slow writing speed can affect exam performance and hinder note-taking in lessons.

Lower limbs

A key example of hypotonia in the lower limbs is flat feet (pes planus). A flatness of feet and weakness in the lower limb muscles can affect motor skills, making it difficult to run (and to walk) with an ensuing difficulty in participating in sport, which can, in turn, have an effect on social skills. Flat feet are associated with hypotonia but there has not been much research into this area. Kirby and Davies (2007a) identified a need for podiatry when researching joint hypermobility in DCD. Recent research by podiatry lecturer Stewart Morrison and Jill Ferrari and Sally Smillie confirms hypermobility of lower limbs and flat feet in DCD and indicates that podiatric intervention is advantageous, but further research is still needed into gait and DCD (Morrison *et al.* 2013). It is unfortunate for the dyspraxic with hypermobility and flat feet that running as a hobby is really not advised and they will probably never be able to run for their lives. PE teachers really need to be aware of the damage that can be done to dyspraxic muscles and joints in enforced PE running.

Eyesight

Although, it is known that dyspraxics can have visual processing difficulties which can affect reading, I cannot find any research into dyspraxia and sightedness. But could the muscles in the eye be weaker too, as a result of muscular problems?

Verbal dyspraxia

People with a specific type of dyspraxia, developmental verbal dyspraxia, have poor control of mouth and tongue muscles, leading to difficulties with speech, and can require support from a speech therapist.

Muscle and joint pains

As a result of problematic muscles and bones, the prognosis for pain for the dyspraxic is not good as they get older. There seems to be a link between dyspraxia and muscle or joint problems later in life. The floppy muscles and overly flexible joints of childhood make it almost inevitable that some ageing dyspraxics will experience joint or muscle pain. Issues could occur with:

- arthritis
- repetitive strain injury/upper limb disorder
- joint hypermobility syndrome (pain and swelling of hypermobile joints).

Joint hypermobility syndrome (JHS)

According to consultant physician and neurologist Dr A.J. Hakim, 'some hypermobile people can injure their joints, ligaments, tendons and other "soft tissues" around joints. This is because the joints twist or over extend easily' (Hakim 2013). Kirby and Davies (2007a) found that children with DCD were more likely to suffer from JHS than non-DCD children.

Repetitive strain injury/upper limb disorder

This is not a well-researched area for dyspraxia at the moment, but it would be interesting to know, for a generation which has grown up heavily using the computer, how many teenage dyspraxics have wrist pain, or develop repetitive strain injuries which they then cope with throughout their working lives. There is some evidence that hypermobility can lead to physical complications in the workplace. According to Arthritis Research UK:

> People who are born with particularly supple joints in the fingers seem more prone to work-related upper-limb disorders than others... A slight twist in the spine, commonly found in people with joint hypermobility may upset the balance between the two sides of the body causing symptoms. (Arthritis Research UK n.d.)

Fibromyalgia

Key symptoms of fibromyalgia include muscle pain and fatigue, so it would be interesting to know whether there is any prevalence of fibromyalgia in a dyspraxic population.

Remedies for muscle and joint issues

(See also the section on *key professionals* later in this chapter, page 52.)

Heat and ice

For the relief of pain, ice packs alternated with heat or heat-releasing gel can be used for reducing inflammation and pain. For some people this can mean salvation from painful wrists or backs, whereas for others, this method rarely or never works. For some, heat works best; others prefer cold. This is one method for using hot and cold for dyspraxic aches and pains:

- Use an ice pack for at least six minutes but not more than 20 minutes (being careful to follow manufacturer's instructions about length of time and protection of skin from direct contact with the ice pack).

- Two hours later use a hot water bottle or a heat ointment.
- Alternate, heat and cold every two hours.

Gym

Regular activity at a gym can strengthen dyspraxic muscles. Types of exercise to strengthen muscles can include:

- stretching
- running short circuits
- balancing on wobble boards and on one leg
- throwing and catching balls.

Handwriting

Ultimately there would not be much value in focusing on letter shapes and styles to improve dyspraxic handwriting without first focusing on increasing muscle strength in the hand and wrists. Equipment that can be used to increase hand strength includes:

- stress balls
- Rubik's cube
- powerball.

Desk space

In a classroom setting, it is quite possible that teenage and adult students with dyspraxia are suffering from physical pain or discomfort, and inevitably this will have an impact on concentration and learning. It is really crucial, because of weaknesses in dyspraxic muscle and joint formation, that dyspraxic workspaces are monitored, from an early age. Ideally, chairs should be at an appropriate height for desks, particularly where laptops or computers are being used, and computer breaks should be encouraged. Unfortunately, the natural inclination of teenage dyspraxics is to slouch, probably as a result of muscle and joint problems, but also because of self-esteem issues. In order to avoid future difficulties with pain and to aid concentration, dyspraxics need to be aware of their posture in a learning environment. Ramrod backs are not considered to be a good thing nowadays, but slouching is not recommended either, particularly when teenage dyspraxics may spend so many hours a day sitting at a desk. (See also *reading environment*, page 71.)

Coordination

Weaknesses in the vestibular system can result in issues with physical coordination. The brain controls different parts of the body so they work effectively together, in a coordinated way. Low muscle tone and poor coordination are interlinked. There may also be problems with 'bilateral integration, the neurological process of connecting sensations from both sides of the body' (Stock Kranowitz 2005, p.76). This would cause problems, for example, when learning to pedal a bicycle. Difficulties with coordination also cause difficulties with motor planning for the dyspraxic. It will be hard to catch a ball or to hold a pen or cutlery properly. They may actually feel fear when trying to climb a tree or ride a bicycle. Difficulties with coordination can have a major impact on daily life and as a result on general confidence and emotional well-being. Coordination difficulties will inevitably have a negative effect in an educational context:

- How can ideas flow when writing if the physical act of writing is laborious?

- How will the peer group react to a child who repeatedly lets the team down in team games or cannot participate properly in a simple ball game?

Fine motor skills

Fine motor skills can offer early evidence of a child with dyspraxia. Fine motor tasks are tasks that are performed with the hands. Dr A.J. Ayres refers to the importance of perceptual-motor abilities for fine coordination skills (Ayres 1963, p.108).

Fine motor skills weaknesses can manifest in different ways:

- Awkwardness using scissors or knowing which hand to use with scissors.

- In early childhood, a clumsy pencil grip and a lack of certainty about which hand is the preferred hand for drawing or writing.

- In adolescence, difficulty holding a pen properly which will affect writing speed.

- Illegible handwriting.

- Inaccuracy when throwing or catching a ball.
- Difficulty tying shoelaces or fastening buttons.
- Difficulty using kitchen utensils or DIY tools.

Difficulty with fine motor skills will remain in teenage and adult life.

Gross motor skills

Gross motor skills involve balance and coordination and often involve both sides of the body.

Examples of gross motor skills are:

- running
- riding a bicycle
- climbing a tree
- jumping.

Speech difficulties

Some children with dyspraxia will be slower to speak or have immaturities in speech development as a result of motor coordination difficulties. This does not necessarily mean that they have developmental verbal dyspraxia, which is a separate condition (Dyspraxia Foundation 2014d).

Clumsiness

Coordination, spatial awareness and balance, all share a role in the clumsiness which is so often associated with dyspraxia, and the remit for clumsiness is broad. Not only do things get dropped but physical injury occurs too. Chairs are tripped over, steps are missed, and objects and walls are walked into. The more severe the dyspraxia, the more likely it is that falls will occur too – balance is lost, the world spins and goes into slow motion and the next thing the dyspraxic knows, they are lying on the floor. Bumps and bruises are, of course, a part of daily life for many dyspraxics.

Strategies for coordination

Practice

Muscle, joint and coordination issues can make any physical activities involving fine or gross motor skills difficult for the dyspraxic. Dyspraxia is not synonymous with lack of aptitude though. For example, learning to ride a bicycle may be difficult, it may take time but ultimately, it is a skill that will be learned. And once that skill is secure, it is as secure as it is for the non-dyspraxic. In spite of any difficulty and hardship experienced while learning, the child with dyspraxia will learn to ride a bicycle just as well as anyone else. Physical activity will, with practice, strengthen muscles and joints and improve coordination and balance.

Neuroscientist Robert Sekular, co-author of a study from Brandeis University into how we learn to do things, believes that prowess in any physical activity is based on practice as well as talent (*Medical News Today* 2007). Paediatrician D. Hall writes that clumsiness rarely results from lack of talent and because it is a learning disability, it is an educational issue. (Hall 1988, p.376) This is interesting because it means that with practice, at least in theory, the learner with dyspraxia can become more physically coordinated and display more physical aptitude for activities which were at first very difficult indeed to learn, for example riding a bicycle or driving a car. Denckla notes that, 'Persons given the advantage of training or overpractice on essential motor skills may enter adult life without obvious difficulty unless challenged by new skills to learn' (Denckla 1984, p.253). This is why occupational therapy can be literally life changing for young dyspraxics.

Are dyspraxics born with an aversion to sport? I think not. It is inevitable that the child who becomes aware that they are not proficient physically at school, and may well be mocked by their peers as a result of their lack of aptitude for catching a ball or running, may well grow up to feel a profound self-consciousness when performing any physical task and have a deep embarrassment about their physical self. The resulting lack of self-esteem can be etched very deeply indeed into the dyspraxic psyche: once damaged, confidence is difficult to mend. The result could be that a child who actually found physical activity invigorating (most children do) but performed poorly might avoid participating in physical activity as much as possible with a resulting social isolation at the playground stage of schooling. The irony is that the child with dyspraxia or adolescent who shirks sport because of poor performance could actually have become a more able sportsperson through practice, which would have strengthened muscle tone, improved coordination and perceptual motor skills, and boosted confidence.

Sport

Examples of sports that will benefit dyspraxia are detailed below.

Swimming

Swimming should be excellent for developing proprioceptive skills relating to body position and movement of body parts. Teacher and author Geoff Brookes recommends swimming because the water allows sequential, planned movement which can be used as a model for other non-water-based physical activity (*TES* 2003).

Tennis

The Vestibular Disorders Association gives tennis as an example of a skill where balance control will be maximised through repeated movements (Vestibular Disorders Association 2014b). Visual perceptual skills should also be improved too.

Cycling

Cycling will improve balance and coordination and bilateral skills.

Skateboarding

Skateboarding is good for balancing skills, but obviously requires a lot of practice, and falls may damage joints which are already weak.

Horse riding

Horse riding is very good for posture and balance. Alexander Technique practitioners (see page 54) use a model of a horse when they are teaching their students how to align themselves physically.

Karate

Karate can be a good option for the flat-footed dyspraxic who might injure lower limbs and weak ankles when doing running activities. The repetition of actions in Karate will help balance and coordination.

Dancing

Dance will reinforce coordination and balance skills and should appeal to dyspraxics who enjoy motion.

Running

One flat-footed student with dyspraxic tendencies, when asked how he had learned to run in the armed forces, replied, 'It was the shouting!' In fact, he had been taught to run by learning to mimic the breathing and the physical stance of his fellow runners, including how they moved their arms and shoulders in rhythm with their feet. Running has to be approached with caution for flat-footed dyspraxics though because of the serious damage that can be done to weak joints and ligaments. Insoles from a podiatrist, tailored to the individual's feet, can make a huge difference to running speed and walking stamina. Probably, for dyspraxics with flat feet, running could never be a hobby because foot and ankle difficulties will remain, in spite of orthoses.

Computer games

In an interview with Richard Alleyne, psychologist Dr Matthew Dye discusses research that has found that video games can develop hand–eye coordination and improve visual cognition and visual-spatial memory (*The Daily Telegraph* 2009b).

Dyspraxic tools

Adapted products can help with coordination difficulties both in the classroom and at home.

Stationery

Adapted pens need to be tried and tested for comfort and versatility. An adapted pen can make writing a more comfortable, easier and speedier process, potentially making a difference to progress in the classroom. A comfortable grip can also result in legible instead of illegible writing, with the possibility of gaining better marks. For students with dyspraxia, rollerball rather than ballpoint pens may be preferable because less pressure is required. Modern technology has produced a priceless solution for the dyspraxic who struggles with handwriting. There is a major downside though: endless keyboarding can damage weak, dyspraxic wrists.

Adapted scissors with larger finger loops can also be useful for students with dyspraxia.

Personal care

Electric toothbrushes and electric shavers can be easier to use than non-electric gadgets.

Kitchen utensils

Jar grippers and wide-handled utensils can be useful in the kitchen.

Cycling

Jyrobikes can help children with dyspraxia, adolescents (and adults) to ride a bicycle because the gyroscope mechanism stabilises the bicycle. This is a life-changing, innovative product for dyspraxics who have struggled to learn how to bike.

Balance: a balancing act

Difficulties with balance are a consequence of other factors of physical dyspraxia, such as poor proprioception, low muscle tone and coordination difficulties. The Vestibular Disorders Association also describes the importance of sensory input from sight, touch and the vestibular system: 'Balance is achieved and maintained…[through]…integration of that sensory input; and motor output to the eye and body muscles' (Vestibular Disorders Association 2014b). Balance is yet another factor which can make it difficult for the child with dyspraxia to learn to ride a bicycle.

The balancing bench

Balance is a sensitive issue for me as a result of a gym class at school, when I was eight years old. We were in small groups balancing along upturned benches. The teacher stopped the entire class of more than 30 children to watch me carry on my struggle to navigate along a bench. Why? So everyone could have a giggle about the child who could not balance, leading to this question: how much do negative experiences at school impact on the confidence of the child with dyspraxia to reinforce and perpetuate difficulties in performing simple physical tasks?

Posture

For the dyspraxic, problems with posture may occur for physical and psychological reasons:

- Vestibular and proprioceptive difficulties can lead to poor posture.

- Muscle and joint problems can put strain on posture, resulting in poor posture.

- As they progress through their teenage years, dyspraxics can develop a tendency to slouch, as a result of low self-esteem. This poor posture can in turn create muscle and joint problems, exacerbating an existing weakness in physical structure.

Paediatric occupational therapist Catherine Williams suggests that, 'Children who slump in their seat, lean against surfaces or people persistently are likely to have difficulties with vestibular processing' (Williams 2013, p.38).

Alexander Technique (see the section on *general strategies for physical dyspraxia*, page 54) can be invaluable for improving posture. Alexander Technique (AT) has to be taught properly by a qualified practitioner. An Alexander Technique practitioner taught me that the neck is supporting a head, which as a part of the physical whole is actually very heavy. This is an AT 'lengthening' and 'widening' method for improving posture which I was taught to use:

- Think about the neck when walking. Think giraffe.

This focus on 'lengthening' and 'widening' tends to instantly result in better posture and can be used as a quick and easy remedy for a slouching dyspraxic in the classroom, to bring immediate benefit to their posture and increase blood flow to the brain so they can concentrate better.

(See also the section on *desk space*, page 41).

Spatial awareness

Difficulties with visual perception and proprioception can lead to difficulties with spatial awareness for dyspraxics. Spatial awareness, or lack of it, can have an impact on many different areas of life: not only is it yet another factor contributing to difficulties in the gym and in PE lessons, but it can affect mathematical ability too. Spatial awareness can cause difficulties of navigation when travelling through a crowded space, using stairs or ladders and, of course, for the adult dyspraxic, spatial awareness reaches an apex of importance when driving. Could difficulties with space even have some impact on the social unease which many dyspraxics experience?

Motion

Some dyspraxics seem to crave motion as a result of being 'undersensitive to vestibular input, and may seek out extra movement experiences in an effort to "fuel" their central nervous system with meaningful information' (Kurtz 2007, p.80). A sense of equilibrium can be achieved through motion: spinning, dancing and swinging. When other people are 'green' with dizziness on the spinning cups at the fairground, and the cups are spinning wildly, the spinning dyspraxic could still be having fun. Rocking is something of a taboo because of its links with mental disturbance but search any dyspraxic forum and there will be discussions about rocking. Rocking can be a sign of vestibular disorder. However, rocking stimulates the vestibular system, so it would make sense that where there is a vestibular deficit, a child with dyspraxia, teenager or even adult might rock, even if it is only a slight, barely noticeable, unconscious adjustment backwards and forwards. Perhaps dyspraxic vestibular difficulties, even in adult life, can be eased by rocking chairs or swing benches? Conversely, there may also be dyspraxics who suffer badly from motion sickness and do not like motion, 'Some children with inadequate sensory processing of vestibular input may be overly sensitive, causing them to get dizzy easily and to avoid activities that involve strong movement experiences' (Kurtz 2007, p.80).

Co-existing physical symptoms

Dr Alex Richardson, founder of Food and Behaviour (FAB) Research, and a leading researcher into the use of omega-3 fatty acid, has found that fish oil could be helpful in controlling some of the symptoms of dyspraxia, both physical and mental. According to a FAB factsheet on SpLDs, 'imbalances or deficiencies of certain highly unsaturated fatty acids (HUFA) may contribute to a range of behavioural and learning difficulties' including dyspraxia (Food and Behaviour Research 2003). Indicators of deficiency include:

- emotional issues
- memory difficulties
- concentration issues
- sleeplessness or oversleeping

- atopic reactions (e.g. asthma/eczema)
- hair in poor condition
- weak nails
- urinating frequently
- visual sensitivity
- visual difficulties when reading.

(Food and Behaviour Research 2003)

Richardson does not expect fatty acids to help in every case and recognises that they are only one contributory factor for an SpLD, but a good response to fatty acids would involve improvements in the indicators listed above. The experience of Paul Shattock and Paul Whiteley of the Autism Research Unit at the University of Sunderland leads them to also support the use of omega-3-based fish oil supplements for individuals with dyspraxia (Shattock and Whiteley 2004, p.14).

While researching autism spectrum disorders, Shattock and Whiteley have become aware through sibling anecdotal evidence that the following difficulties also appear to be present in some people with dyspraxia:

- eczema
- predisposed to ear problems
- bowel difficulties
- sensory issues
- symptoms stress-induced
- certain foods (e.g. citrus fruits) contribute to worsening symptoms
- higher than average consumption of gluten and casein (found in milk, cheese and some additives).

So diverse are the physical and mental symptoms of dyspraxia that there can be a sense that general medical practitioners are simply not making a connection between the diversity of different ailments/difficulties with which the dyspraxic patient can present.

Eating

Eating can affect dyspraxics in various ways, literally ruining their enjoyment of food. There are three ways in which they may be affected:

- Muscular when swallowing and chewing.
- Coordination when using cutlery.
- Sensory issues when confronted with different textures of food.

Swallowing/chewing

According to the Dyspraxia Support Group of New Zealand, the dyspraxic infant 'may have had trouble learning to feed or suck'. It would be interesting to know how many dyspraxics are slow eaters because of oral muscular weaknesses.

Cutlery

Cutlery can make eating slow and cumbersome for dyspraxics at home and at school, and when cutlery is badly designed with, for example, an uncomfortable, unwieldy handle or a fork that is too narrow or a knife that is not serrated enough, the dyspraxic will be aware of this even if their non-dypraxic counterparts are not. They will eat much more slowly, particularly struggling with, for example, peas or rice, and will not enjoy their food as much or maybe will not clear their plate because they are feeling rushed. Learners with dyspraxia may have to sit through afternoon classes hungry and this could lead to inattentiveness. Coordination difficulties can also mean that dyspraxics are 'messy' because food and drink does not always convey smoothly to the mouth, and there may be frequent spillages and food-stained clothing. Does eating also become a chore when cutlery is difficult to manipulate?

Faddy eaters

Gustatory perceptions can mean that the dyspraxic can have particular textures and tastes which they will not eat throughout their life. Sensory issues can mean that the texture of food, for example 'lumpy' food such as potatoes which are not thoroughly mashed, can be literally revolting for a dyspraxic, resulting in faddy eating. They might also have unusual tastes, for example liking their food well cooked to the point of being burnt. School meals can be very difficult because they cannot cater for individual tastes. Certainly, dyspraxics are not 'faddy' to be difficult but because of physical sensations over which they have no control.

Digestive disorders

Is it possible that the low muscle tone that is so commonly associated with dyspraxia could also cause some dyspraxics to have bowel and gut problems? Author and dyspraxic champion Mary Colley notes that 'Constipation and irritable bowel syndrome can be caused by problems in contracting the abdominal muscles and pushing at the same time' (Colley 2006, p.63). Shattock and Whiteley also note that in later life casein may be excluded from the diet, almost as if the individual knows it is causing problems (Shattock and Whiteley 2004, p.11).

How many dyspraxics have dietary or digestive difficulties which they tolerate by adjusting their lifestyle or self-medicating, without realising that these difficulties may in fact be yet another aspect of their daily lives which is closely associated with dyspraxia?

Urinary difficulties

Could weak muscle tone mean that children with dyspraxia are bedwetters, even when they are at junior school? Annell mentioned enuresis as a 'behavioural' consequence of dyspraxia in the late 1940s (Annell, cited in the *British Medical Journal* 1962, p.1665).

Key professionals for physical dyspraxia

Key NHS professionals, accessible through a GP, who can support the physical symptoms of dyspraxia, are:

- occupational therapist
- physiotherapist
- podiatrist
- speech therapist.

Occupational therapist (OT)

The OT can give a valuable assessment and advice about tools and exercises which may be of use in developing muscles (and motor skills). They can also provide recommendations for access to exams. Some OTs use Sensory Integration Therapy, based on occupational therapist and educational psychologist Dr A.J. Ayres's Sensory Integration Theory. This type of sensory therapy is used to give dyspraxics sensory experiences to encourage development of motor skills. Referring to Ayres's hypothesis, academic Nancy Pollock writes that sensory integration difficulties could explain why some children have difficulty in learning, organisation, concentration and social activities (Pollock 2009, p.6). Occupational therapists may also use a perceptual-motor approach, with the emphasis on practising a skill to improve perceptual or motor ability.

Physiotherapist

The physiotherapist can be invaluable for giving muscle-building exercises tailored to the individual dyspraxic's needs. They also have tools for reducing inflammation in muscles, for example ultrasound, which uses high-frequency sound waves to treat tissue. As with every strategy, where ultrasound is hugely beneficial for some, it does not seem to work at all for others. The physiotherapist might also use, for example a wobble board to improve muscle tone and balance or focus on perceptual-motor activities. Mary Colley writes that the physiotherapist can also help with hand–eye coordination and spatial awareness (Colley 2006, p.34).

There is some evidence of the benefits of physiotherapy for dyspraxia. Michèle Lee and Graham Smith, having audited physiotherapy outcomes, found that physiotherapy had a positive impact on a group of children with dyspraxia, aged four to fourteen. They also noted an increase in confidence and self-esteem (Lee and Smith 1998, p.282).

Podiatrist

The podiatrist plays a very important role for the dyspraxic with flat feet. The podiatrist will cast feet for insoles (orthoses). These personalised insoles can make a huge difference to the gait of a child with dyspraxia, allowing them to walk and run with more ease and, it is hoped, helping to prevent foot, leg and hip pain in later life. Unfortunately, although podiatry is available on the NHS, insoles tend to be mass-produced nowadays because of budgetary considerations. Insoles that are tailored to the individual are only available privately.

Carolyn Kates, a physiotherapist at the Boyer Children's Clinic in Seattle, writes that three key reasons for using foot orthoses for flat feet and hypotonia are to:

- 'prevent future foot deformity'
- 'prevent future pain'
- 'improve stability and energy expenditure during walking.'

(Kates n.d., p.1)

However disorganised a dyspraxic teenager is, the one thing they will never forget or lose is their insoles.

Speech therapist

Assessment and intervention for speech difficulties of dyspraxia or verbal dyspraxia involve a speech therapist.

General strategies for physical dyspraxia

Alexander Technique

This is described as 'a method by which we become more aware of balance, posture and movement in all of our daily activities' (Brennan 1998, p.92). If posture is secure and the body is relaxed, then pain which occurs in, for example, the back or forearms can be controlled. The key advantage of Alexander Technique is that the ethos is to learn to use this technique through a series of lessons from a qualified Alexander Technique teacher. Once learned it cannot be unlearned, and it can be hugely beneficial in controlling back and forearm pain, and controlling RSI conditions. Alexander Technique can help the dyspraxic suffering from computer-related pain to alleviate that pain so that they can keep on working, both in an educational context and in the workplace. A standard Alexander Technique exercise for reducing back and forearm pain is:

- Place a rolled towel under the neck.
- Lie on the floor with knees bent and hands clasped gently across stomach.
- Lie like this for 20 minutes, no less.

This exercise is also used by some physiotherapists. Ideally, a book is rested under the head but it has to be the right size, and an Alexander practitioner is the best judge of book size. It is hard to find 20 minutes to lie down each day, but this exercise really is excellent for aching muscles and joints.

Colette Lyons, Pat Payton and Meg Winfield undertook some research at Mark College in 1999 to study the possible benefits of Alexander Technique for children with dyslexia and dyspraxia. The research, conducted using four children, found that after 16 weekly Alexander Technique sessions, the children tended to have greater muscle awareness, kinaesthetic sense and improved self-esteem. Academic performance for reading and comprehension had also improved, although the latter could not be directly correlated with the use of Alexander Technique (Lyons, Payton and Winfield 1999, pp.18–20).

Yoga

Yoga can be a useful tool for suppleness, flexibility, balance and mental harmony. It can also help with dyspraxic muscles, as long as it is practised properly (see section on *muscles and joints*, page 37). Some doctors discourage dyspraxic patients from practising yoga because it could damage their overly supple muscles. There are dyspraxia practitioners, however, who advocate the use of yoga. The Special Yoga Centre in London, for example, offers yoga for children with a wide range of special needs, including dyspraxia.

CHAPTER THREE
LITERACY STRATEGIES

At an international expert meeting in June 2003, UNESCO proposed the following definition for literacy:

> Literacy is the ability to identify, understand, interpret, create, communicate and compute, using printed and written materials associated with varying contexts. Literacy involves a continuum of learning in enabling individuals to achieve their goals, to develop their knowledge and potential, and to participate fully in their community and wider society. (UNESCO 2004, p.13)

Dyspraxia can cause literacy difficulties, but some dyspraxics are dyslexic as well. There are various potential causes of literacy difficulties in dyspraxia. 'Limited concentration and poor listening skills, and literal use of language may have an effect on reading and spelling ability. A child may read well, but not understand some of the concepts in the language' (Dyspraxia Foundation 2014e). Reading can also be affected as a result of visual processing difficulties.

When teaching older learners with SpLDs, however, there can be a marked difference between dyspraxic and dyslexic students, and a distinction can be drawn between dyspraxic and dyslexic literacy difficulties. Both student types may present with reading and writing difficulties but although a learner with dyspraxia might experience visual and auditory processing difficulties when reading, writing or speaking, they may differ from their dyslexic counterparts by: displaying a marked verbal ability, manifesting in a particularly strong vocabulary or an aptitude for the written word. Phonological difficulties may be present for the learner with dyspraxia, as a result of auditory processing difficulties, but may not be as profound as difficulties experienced by the dyslexic learner. Research by Everett, Weeks and Brooks (2008) found that when tested for rapid naming, phonological awareness and verbal span, the results for children with dyspraxia were similar to the control group, whereas performance for dyslexic learners was significantly lower (Everett *et al.* 2008, cited in McMurray n.d., p.5).

Dyspraxic literacy difficulties are complex, and are affected by:

- visual and auditory processing difficulties

- memory deficits

- physical aspects of dyspraxia such as motor-visual difficulties, low muscle tone and weak coordination.

According to Harold Solan, John Shelley-Tremblay and Steven Larson, delays in vestibular maturation may be connected with 'slow vision processing, and delayed acquisition of reading skills' (Solan *et al.* 2007, p.14).

Some learners will have key strengths in literacy, accompanied by some visual and auditory deficits, while others will struggle with all aspects of literacy. For some, literacy difficulties result only from the physical rather than the cognitive effects of dyspraxia. The diversity of physical and cognitive dyspraxic attributes will mean that a learner with dyspraxia might have a 'spiky' literacy profile where, for example:

- Reading proficiency is acquired slowly, but visual processing may improve as vestibular skills strengthen and once reading is secure, there can be a strong aptitude for reading.

- Reading may be sound but memory difficulties result in slow processing and reading comprehension difficulties.

- Spelling is weak as a result of poor auditory discrimination but verbal language strength results in large vocabulary base which the learner may fail to use because of fear of misspelling.

- Reading is sound but weaknesses in auditory processing lead to difficulty verbalising what has been read or researched for discussions or presentations, or there is difficulty finding a fluent word flow for writing.

Certainly it is worth trying to establish where a learner's auditory and visual strengths or weaknesses lie so that deficits can be addressed and strengths developed. A learner with an auditory or visual weakness when reading and writing might have auditory and visual strengths in other areas, for example demonstrating strong visual-spatial skills (see section on *splinter skills*, page 32). It is worth noting that mathematics can also be difficult for some dyspraxics. Nichols and Chen found that an arithmetic deficit is more common in children with dyspraxia (Nichols and Chen 1981, cited in Denckla 1984, p.251).

Vestibular impact

As with physical aspects of dyspraxia, the vestibular system can be seen to play a part in literacy difficulties. Stock Kranowitz stresses how dependent visual skill is on other sensory systems (auditory, tactile, vestibular and proprioceptive) (Stock Kranowitz 2005, pp.156–157). Vestibular difficulties can have an impact on some aspects of visual perception (the ability to process information visually) and this can have an effect on reading. Ocular motor control is critical for the dyspraxic in a learning environment because difficulties may result in:

- visual disturbances to text when reading
- loss of place in text because of eye movements when reading.

The vestibular and auditory systems are also closely linked because the receptors for both systems are in the ear. 'Although they attend to different information, the proximity of the vestibular and cochlear systems allows them to complement each other. The other consequence of their relationship is that if one system is weak, the other may be concurrently affected' (Listen and Learn Centre 2011). Vestibular difficulties may, therefore, have an effect on auditory processing and language development, with an impact in the classroom on reading, writing and communication (Stock Kranowitz 2005, p.117).

Visual processing

Visual cues are actually dependent on other sensory systems, such as the auditory and tactile systems. Teacher Carol Stock Kranowitz writes that, 'Vision, unlike sight, is not a skill we are born with' (Stock Kranowitz 2005, p.156). Key aspects of visual processing difficulties which can impact on reading and writing skills for the learner with dyspraxia include the following areas.

Visual discrimination

- Difficulties in interpreting different letters when reading.
- Difficulties in discriminating between different words and letters on the page to form individual words.

Visual sequencing

- Misreading. Letters are not in the correct sequence or letters may be reversed.
- Place in text is easily lost or lines are skipped.
- Difficulties in correctly sequencing numbers for maths may occur.

Visual figure-ground discrimination

- Difficulty screening out surrounding text from reading focus.
- Difficulty scanning to find specific information on a page.

Visual memory

- Spelling difficulties.
- Reading comprehension difficulties.

Visual motor integration

- There can also be a connection between visual processing and motor difficulties in the classroom, when looking between, for example, the whiteboard and the paper while writing.

Stock Kranowitz notes that we need all our senses to develop vision (Stock Kranowitz 2005, p.157).

Auditory processing

Auditory processing difficulties which manifest with dyspraxia do not mean that the student has hearing difficulties but that they may have difficulties in comprehending sounds and this can impact on literacy. Stock Kranowitz distinguishes between hearing and auditory processing skills:

> Hearing, or audition, is the ability to receive sounds. We are born with this basic skill. We can't learn how to do it; either we hear, or we don't... We are not born with the skill of listening; we acquire it, as we integrate vestibular and auditory sensations. (Stock Kranowitz 2005, p.176)

Paediatric optometrist Dr Jerome Rosner believes that reading is more dependent on auditory than visual skills (Rosner and Simon 1970, p.19). This could mean that, for some dyspraxics, auditory processing difficulties play a key role in any reading difficulties experienced.

Key aspects of auditory processing difficulties include the following:

Auditory figure-ground discrimination

- Distracted by more than one noise.
- Will not work as well if there is a competing noise. At home, for example, television or radio might be a distraction.

Auditory memory

- Slower to learn.
- Difficulty remembering letter sounds.
- Difficulty note-taking.

See *note-taking skills* section (page 86) for strategies for note-taking.

Auditory sequencing

Difficulties with:

- following instructions
- alphabet sequencing
- concepts of time, for example, 'next week'
- syntax of speech – speech may be slightly disorganised or too concise, or ideas may not be expressed clearly. This can also have an impact on writing
- turn-taking difficulties lead to interruptions of peers and teachers.

Auditory closure

- Difficulty comprehending everything the teacher says in a noisy classroom environment because the learner cannot fill in the gaps when not everything is heard.

Stock Kranowitz also refers to difficulties with auditory attention having an impact on concentrating on what is said by the teacher/lecturer (Stock Kranowitz 2005, p.178). However, it should not be assumed that learners with dyspraxia always have difficulties listening or concentrating. Interestingly, audiologist Dr Jay R. Lucker notes that people with auditory processing disorder, 'often look like they have attention problems, but they are attending very well' (Lucker 2012, p.27). Some students with dyspraxia may appear not to listen because they have difficulty in maintaining eye contact and prefer to focus elsewhere visually, while actually listening carefully.

Auditory discrimination

- Confuses letter sounds.
- Mishears words.
- Has poor phonological awareness.
- Confuses homophones.
- Has spelling difficulties.
- Has reading difficulties.

Auditory processing difficulties will have an impact on all aspects of classroom learning throughout the learner's academic life. Auditory processing difficulties are also associated with other key aspects of dyspraxia in the classroom. There are connections with concentration, memory and organisation difficulties. Difficulties with knowing when to speak and when not to speak, will impact on social skills.

For the dyspraxic, however, although there may be auditory processing difficulties, there can be underlying auditory skills. In its employer guide, the Dyspraxia Foundation refers to the auditory strength which some dyspraxics experience, 'Many have good auditory skills such as an ability to learn languages, music, produce creative writing or poetry; traits shown by Daniel Radcliffe and Florence Welch, both of whom have dyspraxia' (Dyspraxia Foundation 2012a, p.3).

Key auditory and visual strategies

Key, easily applied auditory and visual teaching strategies for the learner with dyspraxia include the following:

- Reinforce what will be learned and how before any new theme is taught.

- Sit learners with dyspraxia with visual or auditory processing difficulties near the front of the classroom.

- Be aware of learning styles and make lessons as multi-sensory as possible.

- Repeat instructions and repeat anything taught more than once because it will not necessarily be learned the first time it is heard.

- Write key phrases or information on the whiteboard.

- Angle paper for reading or writing in the direction in which the individual's eyes usually look when thinking.

- Use a traffic light system where a learner with dyspraxia has the option to have a red, an orange and a green cup on their desk (or for older learners, a red, an orange, or a green highlighter). They should keep a cup upside down to show their learning status. This system allows learners with dyspraxia to discreetly and easily communicate with the teacher when they need further explanation or reinforcement of learning:

  ◦ Green = secure understanding

  ◦ Orange = beginning to understand

  ◦ Red = failing to understand.

  (Professor Dylan Wiliam used this method on the BBC programme, *The Classroom Experiment*)

Key literacy strategies

Phonological awareness (the ability to identify, blend, segment and manipulate language) is an aspect of auditory discrimination and analysis that is significant for literacy strategies, even for Key Stage 3 and Key Stage 4 learners with dyspraxia. An understanding of letter sounds and syllable division can be really useful for older learners with auditory discrimination difficulties. Of course, all the key literacy, reading and writing strategies are valid for dyslexic learners too, but for learners with dyspraxia, they should be applied with an awareness that reading or writing may be fluent, but phonological difficulties may still occur because of auditory processing difficulties. Research by Elizabeth Bridgeman and Maggie Snowling has found that dyspraxic difficulties in this area are not at a peripheral level of auditory discrimination but are associated with a stage of processing requiring segmentation and coding of phonemes (Bridgeman and Snowling 1988).

For secondary school and older learners, some of the literacy strategies listed in this general section may seem too basic. But these strategies can be invaluable in empowering the learner because by looking at letter sounds they have difficulty with and by breaking words down, they will have a better understanding of what is causing their literacy difficulties. I have worked with students who have begun to read more confidently for the first time in their lives simply because they have become aware of the impact different letter sounds are having on their reading and writing, and are segmenting rather than being 'fazed' by complex words.

Key words

Although, the average English speaking person has a vocabulary of 20 000 words (Ladybird Books 2014), mobile phone predictive text demonstrates that there are a basic number of words and word sequences which are used repeatedly. British educationalist William Murray and his research partner, educational psychologist Joe McNally, researched words to find that, 'For example, just 12 words make up ¼ of the words we read and write every day and only 100 words make up ½ of the words we read and write every day' (Ladybird Books 2014). That puts an English language system of 400 000 words nicely into perspective and, in theory, should make reading and writing a more manageable proposition if familiarity with word recognition and spelling of the key words can be achieved in childhood. Murray and McNally's high-frequency word lists are still available, re-published by various sources and still used in schools. Unfortunately, their pamphlet on word frequency, *Key Words to Literacy* (1962), is no longer in print. Murray actually helped millions of children to learn to read because Ladybird Books commissioned him to use his knowledge of key words to write its *Key Words* reading scheme.

Identifying difficult sounds

Difficulties with auditory memory, discrimination, analysis, and synthesis can make it difficult for dyspraxic (and dyslexic) students to distinguish between letter sounds, leading to difficulties with reading and spelling. Each learner will have different letter sounds, or vowel combinations, or vowel/consonant combinations that they will have particular difficulty with and it can be worthwhile to encourage the learner to be aware of sounds and sound combinations for reading or writing which they stall on. If a student keeps a note of difficult words, they will quite quickly find that a pattern emerges, which can allow them to focus to some extent on the sounds that are causing them difficulties.

Letter sounds

Vowel/consonant digraph:

> aw er ir ur ar or our

Consonant blends:

> thr shr tw

Consonant digraphs:

> ch wh ph gh

Vowel digraphs:

> ae ai au ay
>
> ea ee ei ew ey ei
>
> ie igh io
>
> oa oi oo ou ow oy
>
> ue

Final syllables:

> tion sion
>
> tle ble dle ple gle kle
>
> ough

Word endings:

> ck ll ff ss ce le ng

Silent letters:

> kn ph ch sh mb gn ps

Hard and soft sounds:

> ti saying 'sh'

ci saying 'sh'

c before 'e', 'i' or 'y' at the beginning of a word saying 's'

g saying 'j'

ch saying 'k'

gh saying 'f'

ph saying 'f'

que saying 'k'

Syllable division

Younger children do not seem to be routinely taught about syllable division when they are learning to read but syllable rules can be invaluable for older learners who are at a stage when they can really grasp and apply this concept to their reading or spelling. Syllable division can be applied to any reading material. Learners can either:

- break difficult words down into syllables because some of these syllables will usually be familiar

or

- look at the beginning of the word up to the first vowel (onset) and the remainder of the word (rime).

When stalling on a word, older learners often hurriedly misread rather than pause to segment the word into smaller chunks which may contain recognisable syllables. This is maybe because older learners think syllable division and segmenting are for younger learners. Breaking words down in this way can be particularly useful when misreading occurs because of letter confusion, as a result of visual processing difficulties. These rules can be useful for spelling too.

The basic rules of syllable division can be taught as follows:

Syllables

- A syllable is a beat in a word.
- Each syllable can be felt when speaking, if the hand is placed under the chin.
- There is a syllable for every vowel sound.

Open and closed syllables

- Open syllables – when a syllable ends with a vowel it is an open syllable and has a long vowel sound (e.g. hi, me, go).

- Closed syllables – when a syllable ends with a consonant it is a closed syllable and usually has a short vowel sound (e.g. hit, met, got).

Once taught, the learner simply needs to get into the habit of applying these rules when reading or writing words that have sounds that are difficult for that individual student.

Resources that I would recommend for pursuing letters and sounds further are:

- *Toe by Toe: A Highly Structured Multi-sensory Reading Manual for Teachers and Parents* (1993) by Keda and Harry Cowling.

- *Alpha to Omega: the A–Z of teaching reading, writing and spelling* [student and teacher's versions] (6th ed.) (2006) by Beve Hornsby, Frula Shear and Julie Pool.

- *A Resource Pack for Tutors of Students with Specific Learning Difficulties* (1992) by Marion Walker (available from www.dyslexia-resources. com). This resource is unusual because it is specifically designed for older learners.

All of these resources do involve 'companionship' though, and exercises probably need to be practised with someone with whom the learner can interact.

Reading strategies

It is interesting that all readers, including those with SpLDs, can usually read jumbled text, as long as the first and last letter remain in place. Writing a letter about word recognition to the *New Scientist*, Graham Rawlinson demonstrates how jumbled letters can be recognised as whole words:

> This is easy to denmtrasote. In a puiltacibon of *New Scnieitst* you could ramdinose all the letetrs, keipeng the first two and last two the same, and reibadailty would hadrly be aftcfeed… The resaon for this is suerly that idnetiyfing coentnt by paarllel prseocsing speeds up regnicoiton. We only need the first and last two letetrs to spot chganes in meniang. (Rawlinson 1999)

Unfortunately, visual processing difficulties are more complicated than merely jumbled text and the following issues can arise:

- Difficulties in interpreting different letters and letter combinations will make reading slower.
- Difficulties in discriminating between different words and letters on the page prevents the reader from forming individual words.
- Text is misread because the eye does not process letters in the correct order or loses place in text.
- Reading is not comprehended properly because of visual memory difficulties.
- Visual disturbances cause letters to flicker or move.

As always, all learners with dyspraxia are different, and visual difficulties manifest in different ways for each learner.

In the classroom, as readers get older, reading material will become more challenging. There are techniques and strategies that can make the process of reading more efficient and more manageable for the learner with dyspraxia:

- accessible text
  - online
  - coloured overlays.
- scanning
- skimming
- topic sentences
- avoiding repetitive reading
- creating a suitable reading environment
- consulting with a behavioural optometrist.

Basic strategies

At school children are told not to sub-vocalise or to finger point when reading, but these are really helpful strategies to aid concentration and focus because:

- sub-vocalisation can aid recall
- finger pointing maintains concentration and focus.

Further basic strategies:

- Never read back over what has just been read, because the writer will tend to repeat their point.

- Use a ruler or pointer, for example a pen, to anchor the text visually.

Accessible text

For readers with dyspraxia who have visual processing difficulties (and learners with dyslexia too), typeface and font are very important. Ideally documents prepared for use by a teacher or lecturer within a classroom will have a size 12 font and a sans serif typeface, as a simple way of ensuring that reading material is SpLD-student friendly. Verdana, for example, is a particularly clear typeface for reading.

Online

Preference for reading from online or paper-based text will, as with all aspects of dyspraxia, vary from student to student. Some students will prefer traditional paper texts for reading. Others will prefer reading from a computer screen. I have found that most of my older learners prefer reading offline to online. Some prefer online. This surprises me for a younger generation who have grown up with computers as an integral part of reading. There are key advantages to online reading, and text on screens is so much easier for the student to control because they can adjust:

- typeface
- font size
- background colour
- brightness.

An assistive tool for the computer is *MyStudyBar*, a tool bar that includes a screen colour changer and magnifier.

Colour

Reading classroom handouts can be so much easier for learners with dyspraxia who have visual processing difficulties if the paper is cream coloured. There is less of a contrast than for black text on a white background. Although cream-coloured paper is considered to be easier to read for people with visual processing difficulties, some individuals will respond well to other paper colours, so it can be helpful to show learners with dyspraxia text printed on different colours of paper to find out which colour suits best and then to use this colour for any handouts or photocopying.

Coloured overlays (originally researched by teacher Olive Meares and psychologist Helen Irlen) can also be extremely beneficial for students with dyspraxia with visual processing difficulties. Again, each student will have a preferred colour. Distorted text becomes clearer with the use of rulers, overlays or lenses. The Dyslexia Research Trust (co-founded by Professor John Stein) has argued that, 'since the visual magnocellular system is mainly influenced by just yellow and blue light, these are the only two colours that will really make much difference' (Dyslexia Research Trust n.d.). Blue seems to lend itself well to headache sufferers.

Scanning

Most learners, even younger learners at secondary school, know how to scan, even if scanning has not been formally taught. Scanning looks for a particular word or phrase in the text and naturally enables reading efficiency, even for readers who are slower to process text visually. The process is rendered easier if the reader looks for the first two letters of the word, not simply the first letter.

Scanning is a prerequisite of skimming.

Skimming

Skimming is an extremely valuable reading tool for the dyspraxia learner. Although skimming aims to make reading more effective, it also aims to empower the student with dyspraxia. This technique has to be used as a 'flexible friend', empowering the learner because judgements are made constantly about when to read and when to skip reading and move on to the next paragraph. For this reason skimming needs to be used in conjunction with scanning. Having read the topic sentence of a paragraph, a judgement is made about the value of that paragraph. A quick scan can be used to check if any key words are in the paragraph, before moving on to the next paragraph.

Skimming methodology:

- Identify key words of interest for a particular topic before beginning skimming.
- Check date of publication to place book's ideas.

- Check chapter headings and any keywords in index to narrow scope of reading.

To skim a chapter:

- Read introduction which should describe content of chapter.
- Read final paragraph to see author's conclusion at end of chapter.
- Read topic sentences at beginning of each paragraph. Make a judgement whether rest of paragraph will be of value. Possibly use key words to scan down paragraph. Some paragraphs list examples or names and this can allow for easy skimming.

'Review' is an important part of the skimming process because this process encourages the reader to review what has been read and notes that have been taken, at the end of the skimming process. As part of the review, the reader can read more thoroughly anything that was noted as important during the skimming process. The review process can give the reader more confidence to pursue the skimming process because text and notes will be revisited and reinforced.

Topic sentences

It can be really helpful to learners who struggle with either reading or writing to be aware of the structure of the first sentence in any paragraph: the topic sentence. It can give confidence to know that a well-written paragraph must follow only the topic of the first sentence without deviating. (See also the section on *writing strategies*, page 72.)

Avoid repetitive reading

The short-term memory deficit which accompanies dyspraxia can make both processing information and concentration difficult and, as a result, the reader with dyspraxia can waste time and suffer undue stress by reading a piece of academic text repeatedly, slowing down what can already be a fairly torturous process. Skimming allows control to be retained and progress to be made. The reader knows that they can always re-read a piece of text later. And the second reading might well be slightly easier than the first. To avoid loss of concentration, which can result from constantly re-reading text rather than reading forwards to new text, the reader can:

- highlight text to re-read later

- use Post-it notes to return to later
- keep a notebook of texts read and pages that may be critical for a repeat read through (this can be helpful for bibliographies too).

This takes the pressure off the student who can read forwards without constantly fretting that meaning has been lost.

I have never worked with a post-16 student who has been taught to skim or, at least, I have not worked with any students who remember that they have been taught to skim. But this technique could be an invaluable aid for younger learners too. The methodology is quite simple and can be applied to any text the student is reading for educational purposes at that time. As with all dyspraxic learning techniques, skimming will need to be reinforced and practised until it becomes a habitual part of the academic reading process.

Reading environment

Learners with dyspraxia are often so wrapped up in the visual or processing difficulties they are experiencing when reading that they do not realise how significant the impact of their reading environment can be. Students can be empowered by thinking about their reading environment which is, of course, an aspect of reading over which they have some control.

How learners with dyspraxia can control their reading environment:

- Holding reading matter an optimum distance away. Not too near, not too far. An octogenarian optician in Liverpool once told me to hold anything I was reading at arm's length from my eyes to prevent eye strain.

- Obviously, in the classroom reading has to be done at desks. But, outside, for revision and homework, students with dyspraxia should be encouraged to read where they feel most comfortable, attentive and productive. This is particularly important for dyspraxia where students struggle to concentrate and have a particular need to be physically comfortable. If they really do produce their best homework while sitting on a bed, then that is where they should work.

- Physical effects of dyspraxia, such as low muscle tone and poor posture mean that the rigid posture that is so often encouraged for learning may be yet another hurdle to overcome. It is interesting that a collaboration between researchers at the University of Alberta and Woodend Hospital in Aberdeen found that, 'A 135-degree body-thigh sitting posture was demonstrated to be the best biomechanical sitting position, as opposed to a 90-degree posture, which most people consider normal' (Bashir, cited in Morley 2006). So learners with dyspraxia who throughout their lives will increasingly struggle with posture might actually benefit by sitting slouched backwards when reading or listening, or even just relaxing!

- Slanted desks can lead to improved concentration and less eye stress when reading (Eastman and Kamon 1976, cited in Jensen 2000, p.36).

- Lighting is important for reading because access to decent lighting reduces eye strain and aids concentration. Lighting should be as glare-free as possible. It is helpful to study near a good source of daylight too.

- Posture also seems to be important for encouraging blood flow to the brain. Researchers have found that stretching increases oxygen flow to the brain (Henning, Kissel and Sullivan 1997, cited in Jensen 2000, p.34).

It is helpful to encourage students with dyspraxia to experiment with where they read best. They could try this checklist at home:

- Still/moving.

- Silent/noisy.

- Artificial or natural light. Which artificial lights work best?

- Where to sit? Sofa or dining chair or chair at desk? Lying on a bed?

Behavioural optometrist

Behavioural optometrists use eye exercise to improve visual processing skills. Once learned these exercises can be practised anywhere and can help with reading.

Writing strategies

Difficulties in writing for any learner with an SpLD may involve:

- difficulties expressing thoughts and ideas in writing (writer's block)

- spelling

- grammar.

Difficulties in writing for the learner with dyspraxia are multi-faceted, resulting from a combination of physical and cognitive factors including:

- visual-motor difficulties when copying from the whiteboard

- motor-coordination difficulties and hypotonia/hypermobility affecting wrist control for writing, making it difficult to write quickly enough to keep up with thoughts and ideas

- auditory sequencing difficulties, causing difficulties with conversion of thoughts into words

- visual memory or auditory discrimination difficulties causing difficulties with spelling.

Writing difficulties will have an impact when the student is:

- note-taking while listening or copying

- writing independently in lessons or for homework assignments

- writing in examinations (see Chapter Four).

Writing difficulties can result in untidy work, with a lot of crossing out. This can be due to mistakes resulting from indecisiveness, as well as motor difficulties or lack of concentration. Writing difficulties can also, of course, affect marks.

Basic strategies

Basic writing strategies are designed to get ideas written into a draft copy. There are no easy solutions for writing difficulties but key strategies are to:

- never be fazed by the word count – build it slowly

- keep writing.

Classroom

In anticipation of written work, it is really beneficial for learners with dyspraxia if the teacher:

- writes instructions on the whiteboard, as well as giving them orally

- allows longer to copy from the whiteboard or to note-take when listening

- allows an arrangement to photocopy a trusted peer's lesson notes

- makes sure the learner is in a position for optimum listening without distractions from other noises
- encourages the student to bullet point key points from a lesson, to reinforce learning and to create a landscape for writing.

Independent writing

The following strategies can help to build dyspraxic writing confidence and to encourage writing:

Environment

- Try to have the best possible study environment which is as quiet as possible if the writer is distracted easily by other noises.

Writer's block

- Verbalise while writing to allow for a smoother transition from the mind to the written word.
- Avoid being fazed by the idea of writing by thinking small initially. Words can grow from:
  - bullet-point

  to

  - phrase

  to

  - sentence

  to

  - paragraph.
- Remember that the writing is always a draft until the deadline day and that it can be reformatted and have academic conventions applied later on. The most important thing is to get thoughts, ideas and evidence of reading or research onto the page.
- Keep writing into draft. Do not stall because the stress of writer's block, or thoughts of a piece of work that has not been written will make the act of writing even harder.
- Establish a word count target for each paragraph or section to make writing more manageable.

Notes

- Try to write straight onto computer. But if writing onto paper really works best, then write onto paper first.

- Keep a notebook to jot ideas into so they do not get lost. Write down any ideas that arise while reading or anything useful learned during lessons.

Colour

- Colour code draft copy to identify texts that can be linked together for final draft.

Time out

- Take breaks and have treats. The subconscious mind thinks about assignments while sleeping or resting, without the conscious mind ever needing to be aware of this.

Topic sentences

(See also section on *reading strategies*, page 66.)

The topic sentence is the first sentence in the paragraph and tells the reader what that paragraph will be about. Each paragraph should cover one issue only. The rest of the paragraph, if well written, should stick only to that point, elaborating and giving further examples. Topic sentences can really help with structure and writing flow.

Signal words

Signal words are transition words that can be used to move ideas and arguments forward in writing. It could help with writer's block for a learner with dyspraxia to have a signal words handout when writing academically. This table gives examples of signal words and their types:

Signal word type	Example words
Time (when)	*presently, ultimately, next, finally*
Illustration (example)	*for example, for instance, this is specifically to illustrate*
Enumeration (ideas in order)	*firstly, secondly, finally*
Continuation (there are more ideas)	*furthermore, moreover, in addition*
Contrast (show differences)	*although, but, whereas, however*
Comparison (show similarities)	*similarly, in comparison*
Cause/effect (show result of an idea)	*because, therefore, consequently, for this reason, as a result*
Emphasis (introduces an important point)	*important to note, a key feature, noteworthy, especially, a significant factor*
Repeat words (to reinforce an idea)	*briefly, to simplify*
Swivel words (changing direction)	*however, nevertheless, but*
Summation (concluding)	*to summarise, in conclusion, finally, to conclude*

Spelling

Computer spellcheckers have offered salvation to poor spellers when writing onto the computer. Unfortunately, not all writing is done on a computer and strategies referred to in the *key literacy strategies* section (page 62) and Chapter Five (*memory*) may be useful for learners who want to hone their spelling skills.

Homophones

Words with the same sound but different spellings are particularly difficult for learners with dyspraxia with auditory difficulties. For regularly used homophones to be properly learned, spelling strategies do need to be used:

- See Chapter Five for *Neuro-Linguistic Programming spelling strategy* (page 122).
- Anchor words visually, for example use a mental image of a broomstick for 'witch', and contrast this with a visual 'wh' for

'which'. Or use an image of 'I' for 'their', to recollect that 'their' has an 'I' when it is about people.

Top misspelled words list

Oxford Dictionaries supply a very useful list of the most misspelled words at www.oxforddictionaries.com/words/common-misspellings, including spelling advice.

Grammar

Learners with dyspraxia with literacy difficulties will often struggle with grammar but it is useful to focus on certain aspects to ensure that an assignment is readable for the marker, otherwise a student may lose points. Some comprehension of certain grammar rules will also ease writer's block too. Key grammar areas to reinforce are:

- sentence structure
- commas
- parallel sentences
- semi-colons
- apostrophes
- writing paragraphs.

Parallel sentences

One of the key areas of grammar that can cause difficulties for learners with dyspraxia with auditory processing difficulties is parallel sentence structure. Often the sense of a sentence gets jumbled because clauses are in the wrong place for syntactical flow, or verb tenses or singular/plural connections are formed differently in different parts of a sentence. Verbs and nouns in each part of a sentence should have the same construction.

An example of a sentence which is not parallel is:

- Some learners find it useful *to doodle* or *having* something to hold, for example, a soft ball.

To become parallel, this sentence should use the verb 'to have' instead of 'having', to balance with the verb used in the first part of the sentence:

- Some learners find it useful *to doodle* or *to have* something to hold, for example a soft ball.

The best way for students to recognise that a sentence is not parallel is to read it out loud, possibly more than once, reworking it each time. If a sentence is not sounding right, this can usually be heard. Reading out loud can also be helpful for small connective words which can be confused as a result of auditory difficulties. If the sentence is spoken as it would be delivered in conversation, often the correct connective will be present.

Writing paragraphs

- Use a *topic sentence* at the beginning of a paragraph. Everything else in the paragraph should be relevant to that sentence.

- When writing a paragraph:
  - use a topic sentence to introduce the paragraph
  - explore the theme of the paragraph further
  - give examples to support the theme
  - finally, conclude the paragraph, if necessary. Some paragraphs will move easily into the next topic sentence and paragraph without needing any concluding words.

- The acronym PEE (point, evidence, explanation) can be used to structure a paragraph and to identify where to use quotations:
  - *Point* – make a point.
  - *Evidence* – use a quote to support the point.
  - *Explanation* – explain the quote, referring to who made it, what it means and how it backs up the point made.

Handwriting

Difficulties with handwriting can be profound for the learner with dyspraxia, resulting from:

- muscle and joint weaknesses
- hand–eye coordination
- posture.

These handwriting difficulties will have an impact on writing generally. According to dyspraxia adviser Gill Dixon and occupational therapist and lecturer Lois Addy, 'The profound impact of perceptual and motor dysfunction on a child with Dyspraxia has an enormous influence on the child's ability to write legibly, fluently and at speed' (Dixon and Addy 2004, p.1). Dyspraxic handwriting difficulties will be evident from, for example:

- unusual posture
- awkward pencil hold
- misalignment of paper
- uneven positioning of words and writing
- variable letter size and use of case
- imprecise letter forms.

(Dixon Addy 2004, p.1)

Dixon and Addy recommend:

- positioning of 90 degrees for hips, knees and feet
- positioning of paper in line with angle of arm
- upper limb and hand–eye coordination exercises
- use of an angle board
- cursive writing
- use of technology
- access arrangements.

Dyspraxic adolescents may hold their pens unusually but Dixon and Addy advise that 'if the grip used is enabling the child to write fast and is effective and not causing any pain, no matter how bizarre the grip, leave it alone!' (Dixon and Addy 2004, p.2).

CHAPTER FOUR
EFFECTIVE STUDY SKILLS

Cognitive weaknesses associated with dyspraxia inevitably have an impact on different aspects of learning.

- Memory deficits lead to difficulties in:
  - following instructions
  - retaining learning
  - retrieval and recall
  - organising and structuring work.
- Concentration difficulties make it harder to retain knowledge and learning.
- Visual processing and auditory processing difficulties impact on reading and writing.
- Planning difficulties lead to indecisiveness and organisational difficulties.

Strategies for study skills and literacy need to be in place to enable dyspraxic cognitive strengths to flourish.

For the dyspraxic, concentration and memory deficits have a significant impact in a learning context and require two opposing approaches in the classroom: variety and reinforcement. Because the dyspraxic mind is easily distracted when bored, variety will help stimulate interest. Slower processing which can occur with dyspraxia means that reinforcement allows a greater opportunity for learning to get into the long-term memory. Learners with dyspraxia can often perform better than adequately, if they are given a little longer to accommodate new material. This is why reinforcement is so important in a classroom setting because learners with dyspraxia will suddenly 'get it' and when they do they can quite easily suddenly become very proficient in topic areas they have previously really struggled with.

The key strategies for teaching a learner with dyspraxia in a classroom context are:

- multi-sensory teaching
- repeating and reinforcing learning
- using visual whiteboard cues as prompts.

Effective study skills are fundamental to dyspraxic learning outside the classroom. If these skills can be strengthened, then application of study skills to academic work ought to facilitate progress and achievement for the student with dyspraxia, even from quite an early stage at secondary school. All the strategies listed in this chapter are meant to be a support rather than a straightjacket. Learners need to find the ones that work for them and disregard the strategies that are not effective.

Variability

> Children with dyspraxia seem to have good days and bad days; it's as if their central nervous systems can 'get things together' better at some times than at others. Tension also has an adverse effect on performance, so don't put undue pressure on the child. (BBC Cymru 2003)

For learners with a short-term memory deficit, whatever their age, there are good days and bad days for learning. When working with younger dyslexic learners, I discovered quite quickly that they would often muddle through a session with me one week, really struggling with, for example, letter sounds or basic alphabet sequencing. The next week, however, great progress would be made and the learning which had been so difficult the week before would be more fluent. For learners with dyspraxia, there are days when concentration skills are elevated or organisation is better managed and days when the mental 'fog' which can, at times, accompany dyspraxia is no longer in ascendance and clarity prevails. Equally, there are negative days when prevarication, incomprehensible learning and shoddy time management prevail. For learners with dyspraxia, this variability is accompanied by an additional burden because it applies to physicality, as well as mental processing.

The more preoccupied the brain is, the slower the aptitude for learning becomes. For everyone, of course, good days and bad days are a part of life; but for the learner with a specific learning difference, the impact is more profound and dyspraxia is no exception.

The 'difficult' days seem to some extent to be governed by:

- fatigue

- stress

- mental overload.

The 'bad' days seem to strike at times of fatigue or stress, i.e. times when the mind has too much to think about or to cope with. By mental overload, I am referring to the busyness, the creativity and the inventiveness of the dyspraxic mind. The greater the stress, or the greater the amount of mental activity, the more this seems to impact on issues such as time management and organisation, or reading and writing.

It makes sense that processing skills are slower on some days and learning deficits, although always present, have more impact. Hence, good days and bad days. The SpLD student really needs to distinguish between quality learning time and quantity of learning time when they are studying outside the classroom, because there will be days when the trajectory for learning will be 'below par' and time spent studying will be unproductive. This is one of the reasons why learners with dyspraxia can baffle teachers in an educational setting, because their performance can be so volatile. Their ability to achieve academic success is compromised at times, to varying degrees, by a lack of automaticity and a slowness to learn. This volatility can result, for example, in an erratic performance pattern where a learner might get 20/20 for a weekly mental arithmetic test one week, and 4/20 the week after.

Establishing learning styles

Learning style is crucial for learners with dyspraxia. If lessons and study are multi-sensory and varied, using a mixture of visual and auditory methods, learning will be enhanced for the easily distractible dyspraxic.

Inchworms and grasshoppers

The dyspraxic mind tends to lean more towards lateral, holistic thinking than sequential, methodical thinking. A distinction can be made between two broad categories of learners in the classroom:

- inchworms

- grasshoppers.

These terms were first used in a learning context by two American high school teachers in the 1980s, who investigated which learning style worked best for dyslexic learners (Bath and Knox 1984).

Inchworms:

- are methodical
- are procedure-based
- learn sequentially
- focus on detail.

Grasshoppers:

- are lateral, holistic thinkers
- approach their work in a more random way
- use alternative methods of problem-solving
- use a greater variety of methods than inchworms.

I would predict that many dyspraxics are predisposed to be grasshoppers because of the dyspraxic strength in lateral, inventive thinking.

Different learning types

Key learning types, known as VAK (Barbe and Swassing 1979) are:

- visual
- auditory
- kinaesthetic.

These types represent learning preferences for:

- looking
- listening
- tactile or physically active learning.

There is also a VARK model of learning which adds learners who prefer to learn through reading and writing to the VAK mix. It is commonly believed that 65 per cent of learners are predominantly visual. Some learners are an equal balance between visual and kinaesthetic. Statistically, fewer learners are predominantly auditory (between 10 per cent and 30 per cent), which is ironic given that traditionally education involves a lot of listening for the learner. In my experience, learners with dyspraxia may well be less inclined to learn in a kinaesthetically dexterous way as their predominant learning style, but this does not necessarily mean that they do not learn from physical practice. Also, learners with dyspraxia may like to learn while in motion.

When assessed for learning style, some learners are found to use all three learning styles equally, but most will have a dominant learning style. This does not mean that learners do not benefit from using a mix of learning styles. And it would be impossible for anyone teaching a large group of students with lots of different learning styles to tailor the learning individually. There are distinguishing characteristics associated with each learning style, which will be apparent in the classroom and which can, to some extent, be accommodated through a balanced mixture of teaching styles. Awareness of learning styles can be particularly helpful for the learner with dyspraxia outside the classroom.

Visual learners:

- remember things which have been seen

- spell visually

- daydream

- learn well from diagrams, illustrations, flipcharts and the electronic whiteboard.

Auditory learners:

- talk or sing to themselves

- are distracted by other noises when they are trying to listen

- may be articulate

- remember by repeating out loud

- are good listeners

- avoid eye contact

- spell by sounding out the word

- learn best from lectures or when a teacher is talking to the class

- may comprehend better when reading out loud or using dictation software, for example, *Read & Write*.

Kinaesthetic learners tend to:

- remember through hands-on learning

- fidget

- enjoy physical activity

- find it difficult to sit through a lesson
- want to doodle or have something to hold, such as a soft ball, or some modelling clay to mould
- read and think with greater clarity while in motion.

Although learners with dyspraxia may have visual or auditory processing difficulties, this should not imply that they do not have auditory or visual strengths. Learners with dyspraxia, like any learners, will benefit from a mixture of styles. They can be auditory learners but if learning is too auditory or auditory for too long, their thoughts are likely to drift and they are more likely to be distracted or lose concentration without some visual stimulus to break the potential tedium of listening to one human voice for a long period of time. Learners with dyspraxia will often avoid eye contact, listening more readily when focusing elsewhere. Lack of eye contact from a learner with dyspraxia does not mean that they are being rude or not concentrating. If eye contact is forced, they may be less likely to listen.

Tools which are worth allowing in the classroom for a dyspraxic are:

- voice recorder to record speech-based lessons, so that slowness of note-taking is not a hindrance
- digital camera to record anything which needs to be learned kinaesthetically.

Doodling is also a useful 'tool' for enhancing concentration.

There are plenty of questionnaires to establish learning styles (see, for example, University of Hull n.d. (b)) There are also models other than the VAK/VARK model. A quick way to establish VAK learning style is based on neuro-linguistic eye movements (developed by Richard Bandler and John Grinder in the 1970s):

- Ask the learner what they ate for breakfast.
- Watch where they look:
  - Looking outwards and upwards to the right or the left can indicate that a learner is predominantly visual.
  - Looking more inwards, to the right or the left, tends to indicate that a learner is more auditory.
  - Looking forwards and downwards tends to indicate that a learner is more kinaesthetic.

Most people tend to look in a particular direction when thinking. Awareness of eye focus is a very useful tool, because dyspraxic concentration can be enhanced if paper (or books) for reading and writing are placed at the angle in which the eye looks when thinking.

Study skills 'melting pot'

I am not an advocate of deadline extensions for homework or coursework as an aid for any learners with SpLDs, because the more extra time they have, the more they will lag behind on subsequent assignments. For the learner with dyspraxia, the following study skills strategies will help to underpin work in the classroom or in an FE or HE study environment and should ensure that progress in formal lessons or sessions is smoother:

- note-taking skills
- structured assignment planning
- research strategies
- reading strategies
- writing strategies
- time management and organisation strategies
- thinking skills
- examination strategies.

These strategies are really all about tapping into existing aptitudes and are important because of difficulties dyspraxics may experience in:

- literacy
- planning
- organisation
- retention of learning.

Assistive technology resources are also discussed at the end of the chapter. (See Chapter Three for *literacy strategies* and Chapter Five for *memory strategies*.)

Note-taking skills

Note-taking is particularly difficult for students with dyspraxia because muscle tone, joint hypermobility and poor coordination will often result in slow handwriting and discomfort when holding a pen. There may also be concentration or comprehension difficulties. Note-taking difficulties can arise for:

- lesson/lecture note-taking
- note-taking when reading/researching.

Lesson/lecture note-taking

It can be extremely useful for the teacher or lecturer to provide guided notes, for example a handout with *PowerPoint* slides or a handout with the structure and themes of the lesson. This is particularly helpful for learners with dyspraxia because they then have a map of the key points the teacher will make. And they have less writing to do because they can jot any additional key points into the guided framework which has already been written for them.

In the absence of guided notes, here are some key tips for note-taking:

- If *PowerPoint* is being used or guided notes are available, it is useful for the teacher to remind students with dyspraxia of this at the beginning of the lesson so that they do not unnecessarily duplicate notes.

- For dyspraxics, who so often have handwriting difficulties which lead to slow and illegible writing, it might be better to use a laptop for note-taking. (Unfortunately, students with dyspraxia might be more susceptible to wrist problems and may need to maintain a balance between notebook writing and keyboarding.)

- If a laptop is not available, lined A4 notebooks are best, to allow for a better overview of lesson/lecture structure afterwards. It is better to write on only one side of the paper so sheets can be laid out and the direction of the lesson/lecture can be seen quickly afterwards.

- Pages need to be numbered so they do not get muddled.

- A column or margin on the left side of the paper can be useful, allowing notes to be added later and headings, sub-themes and topic changes to be added to the column after the lesson or lecture.

- It is helpful to leave a line gap between each new point, so that the notes are not too crammed.

- For dyspraxics whose writing is very slow due to manual dexterity issues, an abbreviation system can be devised with the same abbreviations always being used. (Random abbreviations will not work because the student will forget their meaning.)

- Notes should be read as soon as possible to assist with recall and reinforcement of learning, otherwise it is possible that new learning will not be retained due to short-term memory difficulties and the struggle of trying to write to keep up with the teaching flow.

Examples of abbreviation techniques that can be used for note-taking are:

- Use initials for key themes.

- Leave out connectives and verbs where possible.

- Use common symbols
  - '+' = 'and'
  - ∴ = 'therefore'
  - ∵ = 'because'
  - → = 'leads to'.

- Use Latin symbols, 'cf.' for compare or 'n.b'. for 'note well'.

- Omitting vowels and consonants from the middle of words will often leave enough information to indicate the full word; for example 'sth' for 'something'.

- Use the first syllable of the word, for example 'resp' for 'respiratory', or the first syllable and the first letter of the second syllable, for example 'hist' for 'history'.

A well-regarded formal note-taking system is the Cornell System (devised in the 1950s by Walter Pauk, an education lecturer at Cornell University).

Note-taking when reading/researching

- When note-taking for reading or research, there is obviously more flexibility in terms of writing speed, so writing can be more legible.

- To avoid repetitive writing (and aching wrists), it is helpful to encourage learners with dyspraxia not to overwrite. So, where a source is easily available to be reviewed online, notes do not need to be taken (common sense, yes, but not necessarily for a teenager who is anxious about being in control of all the information they might need for a written assignment or exam). Website addresses can be jotted down for future reference.

- Post-it notes can be used for ideas, and index cards can be used for quotes. Colour coding can help to sequence thoughts.

- A notebook can be carried at all times, even kept beside the bed at night because lateral-thinking dyspraxics will often be 'buzzing' with ideas but these thoughts can be quickly forgotten due to idea overload.

For both types of note-taking, dyspraxics who are predominantly visual learners will also benefit from colour coding different themes and topics. This helps with reinforcement and organisation of information learned. Also, where the dyspraxic is more visual, concentration and retention can be aided by creating visual associations for learning. The mind will remain more attentive if the learner tries to associate learning with existing knowledge, something for which dyspraxics should have an aptitude.

Non-linear note-taking

Dyspraxic 'grasshopper', lateral-thinking learners could well benefit from non-linear note-taking. Instead of methodically writing in a traditional, linear way, they might benefit from creating more of a mind-mapped effect for their notes, with key themes and sub-notes written more randomly on a horizontal piece of paper. This will allow them to learn in their preferred way, seeing links and associations to reinforce their learning.

Strategies for assignment planning

Assignments benefit from organisation and planning, as well as clever thinking skills. Learners with dyspraxia can be disadvantaged as a result of difficulties in application to task, organisation and planning, and also slower processing skills. If they receive some guidance in methods which can be applied when they are preparing work, then this guidance can become reinforced through practice and can become a useful basis for how to approach academic work.

Approaching brief

The learner with dyspraxia may need to properly understand a brief as soon as possible because of potential:

- perceptual difficulties
- organisational difficulties.

Strategies for approaching a brief:

- As a teaching strategy, it is helpful with a spoken brief to repeat the brief visually on the whiteboard and verbally more than once, because when receiving instructions, learners with dyspraxia can be diverted from what a teacher/lecturer actually wants them to do and, initially, may not fully understand the brief.

- Ensure the due date is recorded and the number of days/weeks remaining is established as soon as the brief is set. Create a schedule of work to balance time when the brief will be worked on with the time requirements of other current assignments.

- Learners with dyspraxia can have a tendency to miss important information when first reading a brief so the brief should be read more than once in case any nuances have been missed or any sweeping errors of judgement in interpretation have occurred.

- Highlighting key words and themes in the brief can be helpful for focusing thoughts.

- A guide to verbs used in assignment briefings can help to avoid questions being answered in the wrong way (see below).

- Learners can also benefit from having a copy of the brief beside them whenever they are working on it so that they do not digress.

- Students with dyspraxia should always be encouraged to ask if they do not understand a brief, or are struggling with the structure of an assignment.

Key verbs in questions

In order to avoid misunderstandings about method, an understanding of definitions for standard verbs which appear in questions is of key importance:

Analyse – take the main ideas and investigate them thoroughly, looking at interrelationships.

Compare – look for similarities between the main ideas.

Contrast – look for differences between the main ideas.

Define – give the meaning of a word, phrase or concept.

Discuss – write about the various points of view, for and against an argument.

Examine/explore – investigate an argument or idea in detail, looking at different perspectives.

Explain to what extent – give ideas for and against a subject, comparing and contrasting them.

Illustrate – give an example or examples to justify an argument or demonstrate an idea.

List – list reasons or facts relating to a theme.

Outline – give the main features of a subject without going into detail.

State – give facts briefly and concisely.

Summarise – give basic facts without going into detail.

An understanding of these verbs will also help the dyspraxic to understand whether brevity or detail is required.

Spidergrams

Spidergrams (spider diagrams) should, in theory, lend themselves to the dyspraxic, 'grasshopper' mind, allowing information to be presented and processed in a non-linear way. This type of technique is probably better suited to visual than to auditory learners. Spider diagrams are an ancient technique, commonly referred to as mind maps, but they are not really mind maps at all because they are a more random tool, lacking the stepped method of mind maps (a term introduced and popularised by Tony Buzan in the 1970s). Learners seem to either love or hate spider diagram techniques though, with no ambivalence in between. So it can help for learners to be aware of them but use should never be forced. The diagrams can also be colour coded to organise and enhance learning.

Spider diagrams can be used for different purposes:

- Brainstorming for ideas at the beginning of a project.
- Planning and structuring written work.

Essay planning

Having approached the brief and made sure it is understood, and that time is being organised to avoid thinking being compromised by a rush at the end, the essay planning stage needs to be methodical because a clever response to a question can easily become lost if the information is not planned and organised properly.

To give essays structure, keywords highlighted at the 'approaching the brief' stage can be used to form a skeleton plan comprising:

- Introduction

- o Introducing the essay content. This can be written after the other paragraphs in the essay have been completed.

- Paragraphs
  - o Preliminary paragraphs can be structured to show theory and examples, while later paragraphs may contain case studies as examples of the essay topic theory in practice.
  - o To avoid digressing from the brief, constantly refer back to the question. (A 'Post-it' note with the question can be created on the computer desktop and dragged into the document, so the title is easily available at all times.)

- Conclusion
  - o Concluding points can be taken from conclusions reached in each paragraph, but the conclusion should also reflect the overall concluding thoughts that have been reached as a result of writing the essay.

It can also be useful to break down the word count between paragraphs to make writing more manageable.

Anxious students with dyspraxia need to be aware that their work is always a draft until the day it is due. Paragraphs can move round endlessly if the sequence does not seem right, and words and ideas are changeable and can keep developing. Indecisiveness can also be part of the dyspraxic mental landscape because of perceptual difficulties and lack of confidence, so students need to understand that ideas may fit into more than one paragraph and the control of the content is theirs.

Final essay copy

Formatting details can easily be forgotten by a learner with dyspraxia who has been caught up with the content and structure of their work. Guidance for formatting includes:

- Follow any formatting guidelines for typeface, font size and line spacing.
- Add header/footer to the essay with name, course name, tutor name and date.
- Paginate the essay.

Research strategies

(See also the *note-taking* section earlier in this chapter, page 86.)

If students with dyspraxia are shown how to research properly, and these research strategies are reinforced, then they will develop the potential to have strong research skills to support their written work. If they are not taught how to research properly, then they may undermine the content of their work by searching in a more random, erratic way.

Key strategies for research

- A broad variety of book, journal and internet sources should be researched.

- Some dyspraxics will feel 'awkward' about visiting unfamiliar environments. Visits to the library for study need to be strongly encouraged, so it becomes a habitual environment for the student with dyspraxia. A learning 'buddy' can be a helpful ally for initial research trips to the library.

- To avoid digression from the brief, two questions which should be asked constantly are:

  ○ Is this research valid?

  ○ Is this research academic enough?

- Research references must always, always be noted immediately, because tracking references down later can be a very irritating, time-consuming process.

- If a notebook is used, colour-coded or numbered notes can assist with organisation of text so that research can be worked into the essay structure methodically.

- Students should know when to stop and consolidate research into writing, then identify gaps and research some more.

It can be difficult for the dyspraxic to understand new concepts when they are first taught. This is why reinforced learning is such a luxury. Research which is able to discriminate and find the best sources can be an additional strategy for the learner with dyspraxia to use when they have not understood something in class because there are so many different ways in which knowledge can be delivered over the internet.

SEARCH STRATEGIES

The aptitude of the dyspraxic mind for rigorous attention to detail should be well suited to researching in this way:

- Begin by making a list of different search terms to use.
- Avoid connectives and stick to the key terms to make the research as efficient as possible.
- Try combining different terms from the search terms list to enhance the search results.
- Each new piece of relevant research may provide more search term leads.
- Search a variety of search engines.
- Search newspaper archives.
- Search topic-specific journals online.

Breadth of non-library research can be achieved by being aware of as many online sources as possible.

SEARCH ENGINES

- Google
- AlltheWeb
- Yahoo
- DuckDuckGo
- Exalead
- About
- Excite
- Altavista.

METASEARCH ENGINES (SEARCH GROUPS OF SEARCH ENGINES)

- Hotbot
- Dogpile
- Kartoo
- Mamma
- Surfwax
- Clusty.

ACADEMIC SEARCH ENGINES

- Jurn
- Refseek.

ONLINE DIRECTORIES OF RESOURCES

- ipl2.

INVISIBLE WEB (DEEP CONTENT WHICH STANDARD ENGINES CANNOT ACCESS)

- Infomine
- Infoplease.

Reading strategies

See Chapter Three for *key reading strategies* (page 68):

- scanning
- skimming
- environment.

To maintain control of reading in an assignment planning context the learner can:

- verbalise what has been read before note-taking to help with comprehension
- where useful information or quotes have been found in a book, note page references and approximate place on the page to be referred to later or scan relevant pages for future reference
- create visual associations while reading to focus concentration.

Writing strategies

The quickest writing process is to gather research in stages, writing bullet-pointed ideas, notes and quotes straight into an online assignment draft. Some anxious learners prefer to gather notes by hand into a notebook and then write them up on the computer because they feel that this allows them to think more clearly about their reading and writing, and to feel more in control of the work they produce. If this is the case, even although output is slower, the student ought to be allowed to work within their 'comfort zone'. Strategies cannot be forced.

Strategies for writing are:

- Remember to save all computer-generated writing and to have a memory stick backup.
- Use signal words to move between ideas and arguments. (See Chapter Three.)
- Use topic sentences to help to build paragraphs. (See Chapter Three.)
- If writing is hard, vocalise sentences to get them into written format, then rework them using academic language.
- For final copy, avoid colloquial language, or slang, or contractions (for example, 'isn't').

(See Chapter Three, page 72 for section on *writing strategies*.)

Referencing

The importance of referencing should be emphasised, partly so that sources are always easily traced if they need to be revisited. Older students could be encouraged to keep a notebook of texts read, publication details and relevant page numbers, to avoid bibliographies being a very major chore at the end of a piece of written work. Alternatively, an index card box can be used, with texts read and suitable quotes noted on each card.

The importance of referencing also needs to be emphasised to avoid plagiarising another author's words. Students for whom writing is a trial can have real difficulty understanding that it is not an admission of defeat to quote. Because their own words are so hard won, they can slip so easily into using other people's words, without ever realising that paraphrasing and citing can offer salvation from writer's block. Learners need to begin referencing and citing both for quotes and paraphrased text as early as possible so that this is fully learned behaviour by the time lengthy pieces of work are being researched and written at A-level and beyond.

Proofreading strategies

Strong proofreading strategies allow the hard work of a learner with dyspraxia to be marked to its best potential, without being undermined by weak grammar and spelling, or inconsistencies of thinking. This is a broad array of strategies to cover every proofreading eventuality:

- Leave work overnight or for a few hours before proofreading to ensure clarity and distance.

- Take advantage of the spelling and grammar checks on the computer.

- Print out a draft. Do not just proofread from the computer. Visually it can be easier to see errors in a printed copy.

- Proofread for grammar and punctuation, and proofread separately for content.

- Read out loud because the eye will see what it expects to see.

- Read text backwards to pick up errors from a different perspective.

- Use at least one 'backup' proofreader for grammar and spelling, for example a long-suffering parent, sibling or friend.

To keep track of content ensure that:

- topic sentences tell the reader what the paragraph is about

- new terms have been explained

- the writing addresses the question

- all references are cited correctly.

Achieving results

Students who can see associations and relationships between themes and ideas should achieve better marks, and this style of thinking should suit the dyspraxic thinking style. It is a lack of thought, research, structure and general engagement with a piece of work that yields weaker marks. Strategies for assignment planning can be used to combat dyspraxic weaknesses in planning, organisation and memory, and these strategies, combined with strong lateral-thinking skills, attention to detail and problem-solving skills, should enable learners with dyspraxia to achieve well in their work.

Time management and organisation strategies

Associated with dyspraxic motor planning difficulties, there can be difficulties in planning and organising thoughts. Weaknesses in time management and organisation are fundamental for many dyspraxics. This is why strategies to organise and plan workload, and to organise time are so essential. Organisational difficulties can also mean that multi-tasking is difficult for learners with dyspraxia and they can become 'fazed' when there are several tasks to do. This means that some learners with dyspraxia often perform better when they tackle one task at a time. Fortunately, there is an abundance of time management and organisation strategies which can be tried to find out which methods best suit the learner.

Time management
DIARIES

- Use a diary or phone to note all important deadlines and timetable details, otherwise they will be forgotten.

- Record all dates and deadlines in the same place to avoid confusion.

- Diary or phone entries can be reinforced by moving them to a wall planner, where they will be more prominent.

LISTS

- Use a jotter to time manage each day with a 'to do' list.

- Non-linear lists can work best for the dyspraxic mind.

- Some students will prefer to list major tasks first.

- It can be preferable to put minor tasks at the top of the list though, because they can get ticked off quicker, so that progress has been made and the time allocated for the larger tasks becomes more manageable.

PLANNERS

- A weekly timetable to organise work can be helpful.

- Searching 'time management planner' on the internet will bring up a vast array of blank time management charts.

- If a locker is available, stick a planner to a locker door.

TIMETABLE

- Work at the best time of day so that work is efficient. Unfortunately, some students really do seem to work at their best in the middle of the night, playing havoc with sleeping patterns, which for many dyspraxics are already disrupted.

- Students are often advised to work for 45 minutes at a time. The problem for learners with dyspraxia is that they can easily be distracted during a break and not return to study or find it hard to resume concentration when they do begin to work again. So, it may be better to keep working at productive times, rather than break too often or too soon.

- Quality and concentration rather than rigorous quantity will be the most efficient way of working.

REWARDS

Comfort times and reward systems can be used as compensation for study time. *'If I do this, then I can have that when I have finished...'* According to Pelligrini, Huberty and Jones, time not learning is just as important as time spent learning (Pelligrini *et al.* 1995, cited in Jensen 2000, p.34).

PLANNING ESSAY STRATEGY AROUND DEADLINE DATE

In my experience, with regard to time management and study, there are three types of learners:

- 'Early birds' who always work well ahead of the deadline and often achieve good results.

- 'Late type one' who leave their work until near the deadline, do not have time to work sufficiently, and panic, resulting in terrible grades.

- 'Late type two' who also leave their work until the final deadline, but work extremely hard, late and achieve good results.

For older learners certainly (over 16s) the early type of working pattern can be encouraged but not forced, particularly since some learners do actually thrive on working to a late schedule.

Organisation strategies
APPROACHING WORK

- Think about learning styles.

- Is anything unclear? Do any questions need to be asked? Always ask.

- Be prepared. Plan ahead on paper and reinforce the plan to memory.

- Use a planner for all aspects of individual pieces of work, not just for time management.
- Reminders can be random, for example reminder notes can be stuck to the front door, the bedroom door or even to furniture.
- Sleep adequately at a regular time.
- Eat a balanced diet, including fruit and vegetables.
- Keep hydrated.
- Use rewards and treats.

ENVIRONMENT

- Keep desk area tidy. Tidy after each work session, not at the beginning of the next one.
- Think about how, when and where best work is done. Some students work better when they are not in the room where they sleep.

PRIORITIES

- Check emails. Do not let them build up without responding.
- Use a paper tray to prioritise and keep control of work.
- Prioritise workload. Put any tasks that can wait until another day at the bottom of the list.

PROCRASTINATION

- Recognise that not working can lead to stress. Do some work…

ORGANISING NOTES

- Use separate, differently coloured folders for different courses or modules. (This sounds obvious but learners with dyspraxia will not necessarily be thinking in such an organised way.)
- A folder specifically for homework assignments can help to prevent work from going astray.
- Use divider cards or hole-punched plastic wallets for individual topics/modules.
- Use a jotting book so ideas and plans do not get lost.
- Carry a jotter everywhere and keep it beside the bed at night.
- Use index cards to help remember key learning points.

Targets

- Have a target/objective every time any work is done. Be flexible.

See also Chapter Five for the section on *memory strategies* (page 114) which can be extremely useful for organisation skills.

Thinking skills

Critical thinking

Thinking critically is important for the learner with dyspraxia because it encourages them to use their thinking skills and to engage with their work, avoiding the boredom and mind-drift which can so easily distract them. When reading for an assignment, students should be encouraged to have certain questions in mind to structure their thoughts. These key questions are applicable to any learning, from Key Stage 3 onwards:

- Who is the author?
- What is the source?
- When was the source written?
- What is the main idea or general message?
- What is the key argument or what are the key arguments?
- What evidence does the author use to support their argument(s)?
- Can I think of any counter-arguments?
- What are the main ideas that have been learned from this book/ article?

Metacognition

Metacognition (a term developed by developmental psychologist John Flavell in the 1970s) can also be an empowering tool for learners with dyspraxia because, by definition, it encourages them to think about their own thinking processes.

- Are my ideas valid?
- Is my thinking as rigorous as it should be?
- Do I understand this? Do I need to ask my teacher for help?
- Have I left anything unexplored?
- Am I answering the question?

- Are there any other strategies I could use to help me with this piece of work?

- Am I structuring the work correctly?

- Have I understood what I am reading or do I need to re-read it later?

Examination strategies

For the learner with dyspraxia, examinations can be particularly difficult because issues associated with dyspraxia can have a detrimental effect on exam performance, meaning that the learner with dyspraxia can simply fail to fulfil their potential in an exam situation. In an ideal world, dyspraxics would be assessed on assignment-based performance, not exams. Issues affecting dyspraxics in an exam situation are explained below.

Muscles and joints

Low muscle tone and hypermobile joints can result in slow writing speed. Fortunately, there are remedies for physical difficulties, in the form of access arrangements. (See the section on *access arrangements* later in this chapter, page 107.)

Memory deficit

Deficits in short-term memory and working memory can mean learners with dyspraxia have difficulties retaining information revised for exams, and even where information has been solidly retained through revision, the mind can be so stressed in an exam situation that it quite simply fails to recall learned information.

Concentration

Concentration issues can also become an issue because the learner with dyspraxia may simply lack the stamina for concentrated thinking lasting the full duration of a test or exam.

Indecisiveness

Indecisiveness can also impact negatively on students with dyspraxia in examinations when choosing questions from a selection, or in multiple-choice questions, where more than one answer is available.

Visual and auditory processing

Visual processing issues which affect some dyspraxics can make it harder to read the exam paper. Auditory processing difficulties can make it difficult to find the words for writing answers.

Lateral thinking skills

Lateral thinking skills can become a weakness in exams because the student might incorrectly interpret what is wanted by a question without actually reading it properly, or answer more broadly than is necessary. The student might also come up with accurate answers which are not in the mark scheme (Birnie n.d., p.10).

Organisation

Organisation issues may mean that:

- questions are not read thoroughly
- basic details, such as candidate name or examination centre number, are not entered on the paper
- time for answering all the questions on the paper may not be planned properly
- planning issues might also lead to difficulties with decision making.

If all of the different difficulties can be addressed and bypassed through exam strategies, then strengths in dyspraxic thinking should have a chance to prevail in an exam situation and performance could be enhanced.

(See also Chapter Five for section on *memory strategies* and Chapter Six for strategies for dealing with *stress*.)

Strategies for revision

There are many strategies, tailored for dyspraxia, which can be used to assist with revision:

- Use a revision timetable to plan revision.
- Think about what time(s) of day the mind is sharpest for revising.
- Begin revising in plenty of time – cramming just before an exam may not be such a good idea for dyspraxics because of short-term memory issues.

- Note-take for revision and once the learning is reinforced, narrow the notes down so that bullet points provide visual or auditory cues for what has been revised.
- Use VAK for revision, making it multi-sensory by:
  - voice recording
  - chanting
  - colour coding revision notes onto index cards
  - making mind maps
  - pacing the floor.
- Take regular short breaks.
- Eat and sleep well.
- Know when to relax.

Memory strategies

Key strategies to remember are:

- Neuro-Linguistic Programming visual screen for remembering information
- peg word memory system
- memory palace
- large Post-it notes on furniture
- laminated sheets on backs of doors
- index cards with key, bullet-pointed details
- chanting topics, revising out loud
- mind map key revision themes and topics.

(See also Chapter Five).

VAK learning style is particularly applicable to revision:

- Visual style should work for most learners with dyspraxia. Index cards and spidergrams can be used with colour and imagery. Index cards can also be extremely useful for last-minute revision just before the exam.
- For auditory learning, reading revision notes out loud, chanting or even singing the revision will be very beneficial. It can also be helpful to dictate revision into a digital recorder or onto a mobile

phone app. Some learners even play the recordings back while they are sleeping! Notes can also be played back while walking or travelling on a bus to get to school or college.

- Learners who struggle with concentration may find it helps to walk around while learning.

Strategies for the exam room

Unfortunately, for the dyspraxic, examinations can present a twofold problem because of cognitive difficulties and the physical constraints of dyspraxia. It is not just about quantity of learning retained for an exam but also quality of input in the exam itself, and this is where difficulties may also arise.

Physical logistics

- Know where the exam room is, in advance.

- Make sure any access arrangements are actually in place, in advance. (See also the *access arrangements* section on page 107.)

Stress

- Practise breathing or visualisation strategies to relax. Imagine you are your best possible self, doing your best possible exam performance.

Interpreting questions

- Check how many questions are on the paper and their mark allocations at the beginning of the exam and plan time accordingly.

- Move on to the next question if time overruns on a particular question, to avoid running out of time before questions with the greatest mark weighting have been answered.

- If possible, leave some time for proofreading.

- Read any instructions three times so that, for example, the correct number and combination of questions are answered.

- Read each question three times.

- Turn over each page of the question paper to avoid missing any questions.

- Highlight key words and verbs in questions.

- Refer to the question constantly, to avoid digressing.

See earlier in the *assignment planning* section for key verbs in questions. If these verbs are understood then, hopefully, basic misinterpretation of questions in exams can be avoided.

Planning and structuring

- Make a plan for each question before beginning. If spidergrams suit best, use a spidergram.

- Do not necessarily answer questions sequentially. Answer the questions that look most straightforward first, and leave the really difficult questions until last.

- Make sure each page is named and numbered and that you have the right information on the front of the paper, for example the test centre number.

- If too many questions have been answered, cross out any that the examiner should not mark.

When the exam is finished…move on.

Assistive technology for revision

Some assistive technology is designed for revision:

- *Cram.com* allows learners to create, study and share revision flashcards.

- *Evernote Peek* allows the user to create flash cards and to audio self-test. Questions and answers can be created to aid revision with self-testing and scores.

- A useful web link is *Get Revising* (getrevising.co.uk).

Access arrangements

The Equality Act 2010 requires exam boards to make reasonable adjustments so that disabled students are not at a significant disadvantage.

There are various options available to help learners with dyspraxia to achieve equity with their non-dyspraxic counterparts in examinations.

- Laptop – as an alternative when handwriting is slow or illegible.
- Extra time – for reading or writing difficulties.
- Scribe – as an alternative to a laptop, the student can dictate the answers to a scribe.
- Reader – where reading is slow, a reader can compensate by reading the questions to the student.

Obviously, arrangements available will vary for each individual. Access arrangements for a laptop can be made at the school's discretion, having assessed the student's handwriting speed. The impetus for this often comes from the class teacher who has observed that a dyspraxic pupil's handwriting is illegible or very slow and knows that, if an adjustment is not made, this will have a negative impact on a competent student's exam performance.

Requests for extra time may need to be validated by a professional report, for example an educational psychologist or specialist teacher report. Requirement for extra time for handwriting may need to be evidenced through a qualified practitioner's assessment. For example, an occupational therapist can assess for handwriting and write a report which can be used to request extra time. This process can take some time.

Assistive technology

Assistive technology is there to help students with all aspects of study, and there are some very sophisticated options available for areas such as:

- recording/note-taking
- text to speech
- voice recognition (speech to text dictation software)
- mind mapping
- research
- time management.

Key examples below are free.

Recording/Note-taking

Recording software is particularly useful for learners with dyspraxia who are slow to write, allowing them to record lectures or lessons and meaning information does not get lost in the written note-taking process. Note-taking options are invaluable because, for the dyspraxic, retention of ideas and information can be difficult, but technology allows instant logging of any ideas or information, for retrieval later.

- *Evernote* will:
  - record lessons or lectures
  - note-take by acting as a notebook or series of notebooks, to create and organise notes
  - capture thoughts and ideas
  - be accessible through a mobile device or computer
  - synchronise across all devices, mobile phone, laptop and computer.
- *MS One Note* can also be used for note-taking.

Examples of paid options:

- *Audionote*
  - Can be accessed through mobile device or computer.
  - Records lessons or lectures or acts as a note-taker.
  - Synchronises audio and notes.
  - Offers an indexing tool and highlighter for key terms.
- *Noteshelf* (Apple).
- The Olympus digital recorder can also be used for recording lectures.

Text to speech

Text-to-speech software can be used by learners with dyspraxia who experience reading difficulties, allowing them to listen to text. This software is liberating for anyone with a reading SpLD.

- *Balabolka* reads internet or text written by learner, acting as a reading tool for research or proofreading. Can read a variety of different document types.

- *Natural Reader* is an Apple app, performing the same function as *Balabolka*.

(Example of paid option: *Texthelp*.)

Speech to text

There are two types of speech-to-text software. Mobile phone apps can be used for note-taking, whereas there are other software packages which can be used for dictating larger amounts of text for assignments, enabling the student to express their ideas in writing without struggling with the writing process.

- *MS Vista Windows 7* and *8* have built-in voice-recognition software.
- *TalkTyper* requires *Google Chrome*.
- Mobile phones offer speech to text in their operating systems.

The student will need to practise with any voice-recognition software, free or paid for (for example, *Dragon*), so that the software becomes accustomed to their voice.

Mind mapping

Mind-mapping software can be useful for students with dyspraxia who experience difficulties with planning and organisation because it allows them to create computer-generated mind maps. Not all learners with dyspraxia will want to work with mind maps and a desire to use them seems to be innate rather than acquired.

- *XMind/Free Mind* – planning, note-taking and brainstorming.

(Examples of paid options: *Inspiration, Mindmanager*.)

Time management

The following apps can be used on mobile phones and are an invaluable option for dyspraxics who struggle to manage and organise their time, allowing for instant organisation of dates and deadlines.

- *Google calendar* – reminders.
- *Evernote* – an organisational and assignment planning tool.
- *Errands* – lists (Apple).

Research

Google Chrome and *Bing* offer voice-activated searching of internet search engines and websites, making searching more accurate for learners with dyspraxia who experience difficulties with spelling.

Webpages can be saved to *Evernote*, so that once a useful page is found, it does not get lost.

A general tool is *MyStudyBar*, a tool bar containing free apps for all types of assistive technology software (for example, *Xmind* and *Balabolka*). *MyStudyBar* also includes a screen colour changer and magnifier and can be run from a USB.

(See earlier *examination strategies* section on page 102 for revision technology.)

It should, of course, be noted that all of these assistive technology examples are current at the time of writing. Technology evolves quickly and new apps are being developed all the time.

CHAPTER FIVE

THE DYSPRAXIC MIND
Neurological Effects

The importance of the neurological and emotional effects of dyspraxia on learning, and on life, should not be underestimated. The first part of this chapter covers the dyspraxic memory deficit, using strategies that have direct relevance to the classroom and to life generally. Strategies contained in subsequent sections on sleeplessness and obsessive thoughts, although not directly related, will it is hoped have a positive impact in an educational environment. Characteristics of dyspraxia discussed in this and the following chapter can be so fundamental to the life of the learner with dyspraxia, that awareness of these neurological and emotional issues, and strategies that can be used to challenge them, or simply to cope with them, can be extremely useful and maybe even life changing for the dyspraxic at school, college or university.

The mind games dyspraxia plays

Although there are positive aspects to the mindset of the dyspraxic in terms of thinking skills, there are negatives too. This chapter and the subsequent chapter attempt to identify the different effects dyspraxia can have on the individual's mind. These effects will, of course, vary from individual to individual. Some of the effects seem to be dyspraxic neurological traits (caused by the wiring of the brain), for example obsessiveness or sleeplessness. Others seem to result from self-awareness, the psychological experience of the dyspraxic condition, for example low self-esteem. And there are some traits which could have a neurological and a psychological basis, for example difficulties with social skills.

The box on page 112 shows the mind games caused by dyspraxia.

Neurological effects	Emotional consequences
Memory deficit	Poor self-esteem
Sleeplessness	Anxiety
Obsessive thoughts	Stress
	Emotional volatility
Social skills	

Memory deficit

Wiman and Meierhenry (1969) found that people will usually remember:

- 10 per cent of what is read
- 20 per cent of what is heard
- 30 per cent of what is seen
- 50 per cent of what is seen and heard.

(Wiman and Meierhenry 1969, cited in
Blowers and Bryan 2004, p.171)

This demonstrates how difficult learning retention can be, even without a short-term memory deficit. Apparently, if a learner is interrupted or distracted while using working memory, learning is lost and they have to begin the process again (Gathercole and Packiam Alloway 2007, p.6).

Professor Gathercole and Dr Packiam Alloway record that, in a class of 30 seven-year-olds, a teacher should expect to work with three children with the working memory capacity of a four-year-old, and at the other end of the memory spectrum, three children with the working memory capacity of an 11-year-old (Gathercole and Packiam Alloway 2007, p.7). This shows just how broad a spectrum of learners there is in any classroom, and this will not change with age, making a targeted teaching style very difficult to accomplish.

Learning differences often seem to be associated with short-term memory difficulties, both in short-term memory and in working memory, and dyspraxia is no exception. This of course can lead to difficulties in learning and reinforcing new learning in the classroom but also, for some dyspraxics, general organisational skills can be very difficult indeed. As well as a short-term memory deficit, learners with dyspraxia may also suffer from auditory or visual memory deficits.

There is a curious strength to dyspraxic memory though, because some dyspraxics have an extraordinary long-term memory for small details. Dyspraxia authority Amanda Kirby writes that people with dyspraxia 'may have a good retentive memory, and seem to be able to store information from years before in great detail and to recall it with accuracy' (Kirby 1999, p.152). Students with dyspraxia may remember, for example, what they were doing on a given day or week, two, three or even five years ago. It is that capacity for memory which this chapter seeks to tap into.

Unfortunately, retentive memory strengths do not seem to automatically extend to retention of what is learned in the classroom or through studying. 'His memory may be excellent for some things, but unreliable; he may have a poor memory for either things heard or things seen' (The Dyspraxia Support Group of New Zealand n.d.). The learner with dyspraxia can, in fact, display acute short-term memory deficits. I describe this as the 'candyfloss fog', the tendency to:

- forget assignment deadlines
- struggle to retain revision for exams
- struggle to retain learning between one lesson and the next
- forget to attend tutorials
- forget conversations
- misplace everything – purses, keys, toothbrushes, drinks
- forget whether a pill has been taken or not
- miss the bus.

Efficient memory depends on:

- storage
- capacity
- retrieval.

If any of these factors are deficient, then a learner's progress academically will be affected. And these memory deficits can have a profound effect in the classroom with resulting difficulties in:

- processing and retaining information learned
- automaticity for new learning
- recalling information learned

- following instructions
- concentration
- time management and organisation.

Overloading students with tasks can lead to memory overload. Three key teaching strategies for tackling short-term memory deficits in the classroom are:

- breaking work down into learning chunks
- overlearning and repetitive teaching
- encouraging students to ask when they are struggling to understand new learning.

Overlearning is crucial for learners with dyspraxia in an educational context (and for other learners with SpLDs). This overlearning will involve repetition, reinforcement and revisiting information taught several times. Learning needs to be broken down into chunks and repeated in as straightforward and concise a way as possible.

Memory strategies

Strategies that can be used to compensate for the short-term memory deficit that is experienced by many dyspraxics tend to make use of key sensory learning styles:

- visual
- auditory
- kinaesthetic.

Particularly for visual learning, the fact that dyspraxics may suffer from visual processing difficulties does not necessarily mean that they are not visual or creative thinkers. Some strategies are acquired early in childhood and come naturally without being taught, others need to be learned later on in life. All the strategies listed below can be used to help with:

- retaining information or instructions in classroom/lectures
- general organisation (both academic and general life skills)
- revision.

Memory is very elusive because, in addition to the conscious act of remembering, there are subconscious, long-term depths of memory, and as a result the long-term memory can be incredible in terms of how much information can actually be stored. Although learners with SpLDs often have short-term memory deficits, long-term memory does not seem to be affected. Memory strategies described in this chapter also aim, therefore, to tap into the capacity for long-term memory which learners with dyspraxia have, in an attempt to bypass the deficiencies of the short-term memory. The more random the memory strategy is, the more memorable it will be. Students may well approach these strategies with caution and a belief that they are too random to work. These strategies will work though and while different strategies will work for different learners, once tried successfully, a strategy will never be forgotten and will become a dependable tool for aiding memory, a salvation in the classroom and in examinations. Although examples in this section focus primarily on academic learning, many of these strategies are also applicable to general life where memory difficulties will have a persistent lifetime effect for many dyspraxics.

There are two fundamental memory strategies to mention before multi-sensory strategies are covered:

- association
- exercise.

Association

The most fundamental strategy that can be used to secure learning in the memory is linking learning with existing knowledge. Queen's University SEN lecturer Dr Sharon McMurray writes that associated meaning needs to be attached to new learning because otherwise retrieval will be difficult. Pattern is also important for reducing demand on capacity and for allowing the memory to organise itself efficiently (McMurray n.d., p.4).

Exercise

Research has suggested that exercise may be extremely good for memory. In the 1990s, Henriette van Praag, Gerd Kempermann and Fred Gage of the Salk Institute of Biological Studies found that exercise enhanced the Hippocampus of mice. The Hippocampus is mainly associated with memory (van Praag, Kempermann and Gage 1999). More recently, in a study of memory in humans, Lindsay Nagamatsu *et al.* found that memory does improve with exercise but different types of exercise seem to improve different areas of memory (Nagamatsu *et al.* 2013). Dr Ratey, Associate Clinical Professor of Psychiatry at Harvard Medical School, has also found that a key strategy for improved memory is regular, moderately intense exercise because it encourages the areas of the brain which are associated with memory to release a chemical called BDNF which rewires memory circuits, making them more efficient (Harvard Medical School 2013).

Visual memory strategies

Visual skill can be harnessed to compensate for short-term memory weaknesses. Some key visual memory strategies which can be tried are:

- the memory palace
- the memory room
- the story board.

The memory palace

The memory palace, an ancient memory strategy, is still an extremely useful visual tool to combat short-term memory difficulties. In a lecture at Houston University, John Lienhard, Professor Emeritus of Mechanical Engineering and History, described how in 1596, Jesuit priest Matteo Ricci recreated the medieval European idea of a memory palace for the Chinese. The memory palace is an edifice which:

- is built in the mind
- has rooms containing distinct and dramatic mnemonic images.

The first letters of items in each room form memorable mnemonics, and recollection is achieved by mentally walking from room to room, associating information being memorised with items in each room.

Professor Lienhard regrets the loss of this type of memory as printing processes evolved and a reading society was formed (Lienhard, n.d.).

The modern memory palace particularly lends itself to the visual, creative mind and can be helpful in counteracting the effects of dyspraxic short-term memory weaknesses.

The palace can be based on a real house, or a partially or fully imagined house. Here are some examples of how a memory palace can be used to assist with school or college work, and with organisational skills:

- Items associated with a shopping list can be placed in one room.

- The outline of a speech or presentation is placed in another room.

- Biology revision can be placed upstairs, while English literature revision is placed in a neighbouring room.

- The current 'to do' list can be placed in the basement.

Rooms need to be as visually 'busy' and random as possible, the more outlandish the better. A pink elephant crouching in the corner, wearing purple striped socks and sporting a memory tattooed across its ample forehead would not be a bad starting point.

American historian Tony Judt provides a modern example of the effectiveness of the memory palace as a memory technique. Judt was left quadriplegic as a result of motor neurone disease. In an interview with *Guardian* journalist Ed Pilkington in 2010, Judt explained that at night he builds a memory palace in his mind. His memory palace is modest: it is a Swiss chalet. In each room he places a paragraph or a theme for work he will compose the next day with the help of a Dictaphone and his personal assistant (*The Guardian* 2010). Judt is evidence of just how successful the memory palace technique can be, because this technique has allowed him to deliver lengthy lectures, at a time when he has been paralysed from the neck down.

The memory room

The memory room is a good place to begin building a memory palace. Take any bedroom, with the familiarity of its standard objects – a bed, a wardrobe, a desk, a chair and a lamp. The room can be easily recollected and visualised and the items from, for example, a revision or shopping list can then be placed on the different pieces of furniture, not forgetting, of course, the elephant in the corner. Kinaesthetic strength can also be brought to this imaginary bedroom by writing the items to be remembered on imaginary Post-it notes and sticking them to the relevant piece of furniture.

Here is an example of the memory room in practice, being used to learn the meaning of 'laser' for physics homework:

Imagine walking into a room lined with newspaper. The first thing which is seen is a shadeless *light* bulb, dangling from the ceiling (L). An *amplifier* on the wall blasts music for amplification (A). The right-hand wall is covered in the graffiti word *stimulated*, in different colours and font sizes (S). In the corner of the room there is a pipe giving off *emissions* which smell of diesel fuel (E). Blue gas radiates (*radiation*) from the floor (R). The mnemonic to recall laser is:

- light
- amplification

by

- stimulated
- emission

of

- radiation.

Story board

The story board memory strategy is useful for remembering lists or instructions. Here is an example of how this strategy works:

Instructions to remember:

- Hand in history homework.
- Buy replacement item of PE kit.
- Collect drama script from teacher.
- Hand money for school trip into office.
- Visit school nurse for jab.

To remember this, the following story board could be visualised:

- History teacher is sitting on a chair in an empty classroom wearing school PE kit.
- She is reading from a drama script.
- A purse is open at her feet with money rolling across the floor.
- The school nurse is standing next to her with a needle poised ready to give the history teacher a jab.

That is how random these visual memory images need to be. This visual story board can be played over repeatedly in the mind, like a film, as an *aide memoire*.

Auditory memory strategies

So successful are some auditory memory strategies that they are deeply rooted in early schooling and practised in classrooms throughout the world. Some auditory strategies that can be tried are:

- mnemonics
- melody
- rhyme
- chanting
- dictation.

Mnemonics

A word can be made up using the initial letters of something that is being remembered. MRS GREN is the classic example of a mnemonic being used as a scientific aide memoire, where the letters MRS GREN stand for the seven processes of life:

- Movement
- Respiration
- Sensitivity
- Growth
- Reproduction
- Excretion
- Nutrition.

Another type of mnemonic is when the initial letters of the information being remembered are taken to form a sentence, a classic example being the musical treble clef *EGBDF*, remembered as *Every Good Boy Deserves Fun*. Mnemonics can be particularly useful for learners with dyspraxia who find sequences challenging.

Melody

Number sequences are often very difficult to remember for dyspraxics, and even regularly used telephone numbers and PINs can be hard to retain. One auditory method of retaining this type of number is to hum the number. Outlandish as this method may seem, I have known students who used this memory method long before I ever met them.

Rhyme

Use of rhyme is a very traditional method of remembering and most people grow up with at least one rhyming memory aide. Classic examples are:

- Remember, remember the fifth of November.
- 'In fourteen-hundred-and-ninety-two, Columbus sailed the ocean blue.' (Sackville Stoner 1919)
- Thirty days hath September

  April, June and November,

  All the rest have thirty-one

  excepting February alone.

Chanting

Traditionally, school children have also learned by chanting the alphabet, times tables, spellings of words or even historical facts. Learning by rote involves the repetition of sounds and this auditory repetition secures the memory. It is very effective for examination revision if the learner is auditory.

Dictation

Finally, the act of saying something out loud – a revision fact or a new name, for example – can act as an effective memory strategy.

Mixed memory strategies

Some key memory strategies rely on visual, auditory and kinaesthetic methods:

- Peg word memory system
- Neuro-Linguistic Programming.

Peg word memory system

The peg word memory system is a traditional memory method which uses visual and auditory responses to harness memory. First, learn these rhymes.

one bun

two shoe

three tree

four door

five hive

six sticks

seven heaven

eight gate

nine wine

ten hen.

A visual association has to be created between the number and the rhyming word attached to it, so this memory strategy does require a feat of memory before it can be used, but this extra act of remembering is worthwhile because once secure, this memory strategy can be extremely useful.

Once the rhyme is in place, the list of things to remember can be pegged to it. For example, to remember the following list of French vocabulary:

1. chambre (bedroom)

2. froid (cold)

3. J'habite (I live)

4. heureusement (luckily)

5. commerces (shops)

6. l'escalier (stairs)

7. maison (house)

8. Angleterre (England)

9. maintenant (now)

10. nouvelle (new).

This is how the peg word memory system will be used:

1. A bun in the middle of a four poster bed in a bedchamber (chambre) with the letters 'RE' iced on top to prompt a reminder of the correct ending of the word.

2. A shoe shivering in the snow, saying 'ffffffffffffffrrrrrrrrrrrrrrr' with the label 'oid' on the front of the shoe.

3. A tree house in a tree with the learner waving a banner from it with the letters in huge capitals, 'J'HABITE'.

4. A door with a lucky rabbit foot hanging from it and the nameplate: 'Heur Euse'. Are you 'ment' to knock before entering?

5. A beehive with lots of miniature shops with bees selling, for example, vegetables, flowers and clothes to other bees. A big sign at the top of the hive says 'Commerces'.

6. A staircase made of 'sticks' but moving like an 'escal'ator. As you move up the escalator, you see a sign on each step which reads 'ier'.

7. Heavenly clouds with a house floating on them. The house has three upstairs windows and two downstairs windows with a door in the middle. Each window and door has a poster with a letter attached to it, reading (you've guessed): M-A-I-S-O-N.

8. A white and red gate with a mathematical angle drawn horizontally and vertically: 'angle'. The gate is being moved quickly: it 'terre's across the earth, leaving deep ridges behind it.

9. Now the 'main' 'tenant' in a farmhouse is sitting at the table drinking a bottle of red wine.

10. The new hen is reading a book, a 'nouvelle'.

The peg word memory system can also be used for organisation.

Neuro-Linguistic Programming (NLP)

Neuro-Linguistic Programming (NLP) is a useful visual and kinaesthetic memory tool for people with dyspraxia. Here is an example of how a teacher would use it for spelling:

- Having established which word is being learned, ask the learner what they ate for breakfast. In which direction does the learner look while answering? Is it, for example:

  o left and upwards?

- ∘ down and to the right?
- ∘ straight ahead?
- Ask the learner to write the word. If the word is spelled incorrectly, discuss where the error lies and dictate the word to be learned, while the learner writes it.
- Ask the learner to hold the paper with the word on it at the angle where they looked when answering the breakfast question.
- The learner should visualise a picture image of the word with a colour for the initial letters which precede the first vowel (onset) and a different colour for the first vowel and subsequent letters (rime).
- Ask the learner to write the word again, using different colours for onset and rime.
- Discuss the word shape. Does it have any distinguishing letter characteristics?
- Encourage the learner to draw a cloud round the word.
- Ask the learner to write the word again, but with their eyes closed. This shows visual processing and kinaesthetic skills in action because without the sensory input of the eye, the word will format with surprising consistency.
- Ask the learner to write the word backwards. Thinking about the letter sequence backwards will help to reinforce the spelling. If the word cannot be written backwards, the visual picture of the word is less secure and it is less likely to be remembered.
- Encourage the learner to write the word regularly in a sentence for the next few weeks, to secure the spelling.

This strategy originated in the 1970s with the creation of Neuro-Linguistic Programming (Bandler and Grinder 1979, p.33).

If all other memory strategies fail, there is always one remaining strategy, used by students since writing was invented: write what is to be remembered on the hand!

Sleeplessness

Dyspraxia is commonly associated with:

- wakefulness – disturbing easily from slumber
- sleeplessness – difficulties falling asleep.

Interestingly, these traits are also found on the autism spectrum. Sleeplessness and wakefulness, for the dyspraxic, could be induced by:

- neurological inefficiencies in sleep transition
- sensory factors linked to auditory processing
- difficulty 'winding down' for sleep as a result of a dyspraxia-induced 'fight or flight' state of tension
- physical effects of dyspraxia, such as hypotonia, hypermobility and abdominal discomfort
- stress and anxiety
- hyperactive or repetitive thoughts
- fatigue.

The dyspraxic inability to sleep must be connected to some extent with the alertness of the dyspraxic mind. Although it is a disadvantage to be woken up by the slightest sound every night, throughout the night, might this alertness partially account for the survival of the dyspraxic trait in society? How useful were these dyspraxic individuals in ancient times when wakefulness was key to surviving the night? The instant wakefulness of the dyspraxic allows for an alertness and cognitive productivity at times when others are shaking off the sluggishness and mental sloth in the aftermath of waking up from deep slumber. Could this ease of transition between sleep and wakefulness also mean that dyspraxics rouse quickly after anaesthetic? The wakefulness of the dyspraxic mind could be a strength as well as a burden.

Sleepiness

Conversely, the dyspraxic who struggles to sleep at night can have difficulties in getting up to go to school, college or university in the mornings. The best thing I can recommend for this situation is a vibrating pillow alarm clock to activate when it is time to wake up.

Strategies for sleep

Lack of sleep, in an academic context, will inevitably result in concentration difficulties and poor performance, so strategies for sleep are particularly important for the learner with dyspraxia.

There are many strategies that can help with sleep:

- hazard warning sign
- counting/visiting rooms
- noise acceptance
- deep breathing
- eight hours a night?
- three hours is enough
- regular bed times
- napping.

Different strategies work for different individuals, so (like so many of the strategies that are discussed in this book) sleep strategies have to be experimented with. If a sleep strategy does not work at first, it could, in fact, work with practice. It is certainly worth having an arsenal of tried and tested sleep strategies to deflect the highly active dyspraxic mind from wakefulness at nighttime.

Hazard warning sign

Stop thinking! The endless rambling of the mind causes sleeplessness. When a negative thought or a negative, repetitive thought comes into the mind, a red warning triangle can be visualised to quell the thought. Visualising a red warning triangle can also be used to appease anxious thoughts.

Counting/visiting the rooms in a house

Traditionally, it has been believed that repetitive counting of sheep leads to sleep. Not everyone is numerate, however, and it follows that not everyone will want to count sheep to get to sleep. Another similar strategy (which relates to the memory palace in Chapter Five) is to visit a house, any house, real or imaginary. Each room in the house can be visited, refurnished and decorated. The house can be redesigned completely or a street of houses, or even a palace, can be designed. This repetitive internal designing ought to lull the mind into sleep.

Noise acceptance

Dyspraxia expert Maureen Boon writes that, 'Dyspraxic children can show an oversensitivity to sensory stimulation, whether in response to noise or tactile stimuli' (Boon 2000, p.68). It is ironic that as a result of auditory processing difficulties, although people with dyspraxia can struggle to comprehend what is being said during the day, they can equally have an extraordinarily heightened awareness of noise at night. Many adults will remember sharing houses or halls of residence with dyspraxic or autistic companions: the person who was crotchety to the point of psychosis about noise late at night.

To sleep through noise and not lie awake becoming increasingly stressed out and angry about the noise disturbance can involve:

- accepting sounds, even people's voices
- tolerating sounds rather than becoming agitated about them and abandoning any false convictions that noise makes it impossible to sleep
- aiming for snooze time rather than deep sleep.

For the adult dyspraxic, the baby-rearing years can lead to something of a revelation regarding sleeplessness. Being awakened by small mammals in nappies, without any concessions, throughout the night, can result in the slightly surprising discovery that in spite of severe sleep deprivation, life is still there to be lived.

Breathing

Breathing is key to falling asleep. One has to be relaxed to sleep, and for the dyspraxic individual, the dyspraxic condition seems to lend itself to being fired up, taut and ready for action. If the mind continuously drifts on to the next thought that is passing through, then the endless stream of thoughts can be counterbalanced by simply focusing on each breath. Here is a useful breathing strategy to encourage sleep.

Count breaths from one to ten, i.e. one breath in and one breath out, two breaths in and two breaths out...up to ten. Every time the mind is distracted with a thought, begin to breathe at one again. (See also strategies for breathing in section on *strategies for calm* in Chapter Six.)

Eight hours a night?

Worry about not getting enough sleep keeps people awake! Dyspraxia is no exception. The lightness of sleep experienced by some dyspraxics means that they can quite easily be woken several times in the night and find it difficult to sleep again. According to the National Sleep Foundation, not only do different age groups require different amounts of sleep, but individuals also vary in how much sleep is needed (National Sleep Foundation 2013). That is why it is not really worth fretting about getting eight hours of sleep a night, if six hours is sufficing without causing overwhelming fatigue during the day. A review of American Cancer Society surveys by researchers Shawn Youngstedt and Daniel Kripke found that the people who slept for seven hours a night had the greatest longevity, greater than those who slept less, but also greater than those who slept more (National Sleep Foundation 2013).

Three hours is enough

This is the most effective sleep strategy that I have ever used. It has served me well for many years. The basic premise is this: three hours of sleep a night is enough to survive. If I stop fretting about getting seven or eight hours of uninterrupted sleep a night and just lie awake, literally waiting for sleep to come, without panicking about not sleeping, then I will sleep and I usually get a reasonable amount of sleep. A person who goes to bed at eleven and gets up at seven could stay awake until four o'clock in the morning using this sleep strategy, without worrying about losing sleep. Of course, it could not work for everyone indefinitely, but it can calm fears about not getting enough sleep and help to re-establish a regular sleep pattern.

Regular bed times

Regular bed times are inevitably conducive to better sleep patterns. People who go to bed late, allowing for a minimal night's sleep before work the next day, often tell those who retire to bed early to 'live a little', even although the 'late to bed' individuals are often exhausted during daylight hours. The key is to have a regular pattern for sleep, so that the body's clock is adjusted for sleep at sleep times. There are free phone apps that monitor sleep to show the sleep cycles which occur each night. Based on the individual's sleep cycles and getting up time, phone apps can predict the optimum time for going to bed and getting a decent night's sleep.

I have known many, many students over the years who work all night and sleep all day. For some people that does work really well and they are at their most productive in the middle of the night. For some it works exceptionally well as a strategy for coping with the all-night noise of student accommodation! For others it does not work at all – they become sleep deprived and visibly exhausted, with dark circles under their eyes and pasty faces. But they also tend to become more stressed because the more tired one becomes, the more difficult it is to be rational and the more difficult it is to cope with the minutiae of day-to-day living. Also, the all-nighters will have to adjust at some point to an ordinary workplace day.

Napping

Naps during the day can compensate for lack of sleep at night. According to Laura Barnett, Churchill, Thatcher, Clinton and even Einstein insisted on a nap in the afternoon. Churchill believed that an afternoon nap helped him to think more clearly (*The Guardian* 2011b). Unfortunately, of course, for the sleepy dyspraxic, struggling to concentrate during afternoon lessons, this strategy is something of a non-starter. For the university student with a more flexible timetable, maybe a nap is more of a possibility.

Primitive sleep patterns

Primitive man tended to sleep with naps, taking his opportunity to sleep when there was nothing else going on, just like domesticated dogs. This requirement for eight hours of sleep at night is a relatively recent phenomenon for humans. Historian Roger Ekirch has amassed a large amount of evidence that people used to have a wakeful period in the middle of the night when they might get up and do chores or visit neighbours. There was a first and a second sleep each night, with a two-hour interlude. Ekirch found that this sleep pattern seemed to begin to disappear in the 17th century (Hegarty 2012). This more primitive sleep function could explain those wakeful times that humans still experience during their nightly sleep cycle, a sleep disruption which is even more acute for the noise-sensitive dyspraxic sleeper.

Sleep environment

Sleeping environment needs to be factored into strategising for sleepless nights. The following factors can be considered:

- Supportive, comfortable bedding, including mattress and pillow.
- One pillow may be physically more comfortable than two pillows.
- Reduce room temperature.
- Are curtains or blinds substantial enough to reduce light? Does lighting from outside come into the room?
- Wear foam ear plugs for noise reduction.

Various other strategies

According to the National Sleep Foundation, experts also recommend the following:

- Stop smoking.
- Regular exercise.
- Abstain from alcohol or caffeine near to sleep time.
- Avoid food for a few hours before sleeping.
- Relax during the hour before going to bed with, for example, a bath or calming music.
- If possible, bedrooms should be for sleep and not for computer use or watching television.

Obsessive thoughts

According to the Dyspraxia Foundation, phobias, addictions, obsessiveness and compulsiveness can be associated with dyspraxia (Dyspraxia Foundation 2014f).

It could be argued that for the dyspraxic, obsessive thoughts result from a need to be in control of life, because of the multiple difficulties and resulting anxieties which dyspraxia may bring. However, because of the neural nature of dyspraxia, it could equally be the case that the obsessive thoughts and obsessions which some dyspraxics experience are yet another result of inefficiencies in neural connectivity in the brain. Certainly, it is thought by some scientists that obsessive compulsive disorder is caused by neural circuits triggering repetitive thoughts and behaviour patterns (Graybiel and Rauch 2000, p.343). Unfortunately, obsessive, repetitive thinking patterns will be another cause of dyspraxic inattentiveness in the classroom and lecture theatre, hindering concentration and hampering progress. These thought processes need to be challenged, not only to enable better concentration for learning but to give the learner with dyspraxia some peace of mind.

Obsessive thoughts seem to divide into two specific types of thinking for the dyspraxic (and there is some overlap with autism spectrum disorders, particularly Asperger syndrome):

- Obsessiveness with routine and rituals.

- Distorted thinking can occur in relation to past events and conversations, and these thoughts can be repeated obsessively.

Obsession with routine

Anchors of routine and order in everyday life are a perfectly natural way of coping with the chaos which dyspraxia brings. However, there are times when a fear of change can have an impact on living life to the full and on the future, and this is when a dedication to order and routine should be challenged.

For the dyspraxic mindset, times of transition can be stressful. This would encompass the inevitable transitions that occur during adolescence and early adult life, with change from:

- junior to secondary school

- secondary school to sixth-form or FE college

- college to university

- further or higher education to the workplace.

In Anne Tyler's novel, *Searching for Caleb*, the heroine always tells people to 'Change …Take the change. Always change' (Tyler 1992, p.29). 'Make a change' is a useful mantra for the change-averse dyspraxic to consider because change and destiny are intertwined. Changes, both major and minor, can lead to more life opportunities, and the more change is embraced, the more dynamic life can become. For dyspraxics at secondary school, the positivity of change has to be acknowledged and sensitivity to change discussed – change needs to be embraced, but prepared for in advance as well. And however 'scary' some of the unavoidable transitions of adolescence might be, these changes of habitat, academic environment and social groupings can be positively life affirming. Without such change, adult life for the change-averse dyspraxic could be a very dull, colourless affair, and that could give real cause for persistent depression.

Repetitive thinking

Scottish musician and co-founder of the Scottish Dyspraxion Roy Moller gives an extremely apt description of repetitive dyspraxic thinking: 'The dyspraxic mind tends to "riff" on people's remarks, examining the implications of what they're saying, honing in on cliché, like a habitually zealous customs officer – waving very little through unexamined' (Moller n.d.). This can mean that while a situation or conversation is occurring, it can seem perfectly acceptable, friendly and harmless and does not require a negative or combative reaction. However, a few hours later or even the next day, the dyspraxic mind will often begin to dwell on one thing that was said, that maybe did cause discomfort at the time, and that interaction will be treated separately from the context in which it was said or the outcome of the conversation. The mind will keep thinking back to the conversation endlessly, until another conversation or incident takes its place, to feed the dyspraxic brain's seemingly endless desire for anxiety and disturbance.

Strategies for dealing with repetitive thinking

This overly officious and inaccurate conversation monitor which exists solely in the dyspraxic's mind can be manipulated and challenged by using the following strategies:

- Thought recognition
- Memory manipulation
- Accept things as they are
- Visualisation – film format.

Thought recognition

The 'riffing' aspect of the dyspraxic mind tends to move from being offended by one person, to being offended by another person, so it is important to adopt a more reflective stance and to learn to recognise these negative thinking patterns as soon as they occur (and for the dyspraxic, they can occur very frequently). The tendency to be an over-zealous customs officer with the events of daily life can be used to advantage. Thoughts can be monitored as they occur. Whenever a repetitive, negative thought comes to mind, it can be banished by the thought: *I will think about this later.*

Psychologist Laurence Hirschberg's 2013 article entitled 'Do you have your thoughts, or do your thoughts have you?' describes how every time a thought or action is repeated neural connections are strengthened and are then more likely to recur, 'Like well worn paths in the woods' (Hirschberg 2013). Unfortunately, in an endless 'Catch-22', neural pathways will be set up in the dyspraxic mind, exacerbating anxieties and negative thinking. Hirschberg offers an easy and effective solution to challenge negative thoughts, simply by recognising repetitive thought patterns and moving the mind into the present moment. By moving, 'what you are feeling, sensing, or experiencing, you are starting to build a new path' (Hirschberg 2013).

Several hours after any social interaction or day at work, school or university, the mind may well begin its habitual 'riff' about something that was said or done. However, if Hirschberg's approach is adopted, then the mind can become accustomed to recognising and dismissing negative, repetitive thinking patterns, in the same way as it becomes accustomed to repeating certain thoughts. Negative thoughts can be dismissed repeatedly until a more positive thought occurs in the mind's endless narrative, and although negative thoughts will always recur, it is empowering to understand that mental control can be exerted over this type of thinking.

Memory manipulation

The past is finished, it cannot be changed and one person's perspective on a memory, including a conversation, is always different from another person's memory. When reflecting negatively on a conversation or incident, it is worth asking:

- How much has the dyspraxic mind distorted the original conversation or incident in the several hours after it occurred?

- How much out of context has the incident been taken?

When fretting about something that has happened, certain thinking strategies can be useful for reframing the context:

- Revisit the memory of an event in context. Think about everything that happened, without simply isolating one incident or a few stray words.

- Focus on positive recollections of the memory or the person involved.

- It is easy to take offence but, in fact, everyone says the 'wrong' thing or something they do not really mean or have not had a chance to think through properly.

Accept things as they are

Be stoical. This ancient philosophy can be used to dyspraxic advantage. Instead of negative, critical thinking about things, even quite minor things, that have happened or situations that have occurred, stoicism encourages greater acceptance of what life brings. It is reassuring to know that even in ancient times people suffered from the same mental difficulties as modern man.

- In the first century AD, Epictetus wrote, 'Men are disturbed not by things, but by the views which they take of things' (Epictetus 2014, v.5).

- Roman Emperor and philosopher Marcus Aurelius wrote, 'Put from you the belief that "I have been wronged", and with it will go the feeling. Reject your sense of injury, and the injury itself disappears' (Aurelius 2004, p.31).

Visualisation – film format

Visualisation strategies can be used for controlling distorted memories of events and conversations. When recollecting an event or a conversation and giving it that 'spin' which the dyspraxic mind so often gives, it can be useful to revisualise what happened, as if watching a film and seeing oneself in the third person. It can, in fact, be a revelation to realise that not everyone recollects in the first person. Neuro-Linguistic Programming (NLP) (developed by Richard Bandler and John Grinder in the 1970s) recognises that many people remember scenes from their lives as if they are watching themselves in a film. Inevitably, remembering in the third person is a more detached, less involved way of re-experiencing the past and hence a useful skill to learn for the hypersensitive dyspraxic person who might be unaccustomed to anything other than first-person thinking.

Some other strategies for tackling negative, repetitive thinking are:

- To never look back and reflect on the past.

- Mindfulness meditation. (See the section on *strategies for calm* in Chapter Six.)

- Hazard warning sign. (See the section on *strategies for sleep* earlier in this chapter.)

CHAPTER SIX
THE DYSPRAXIC MIND
Emotional Consequences

As the brain evolves in teenage and early adult life, dyspraxia seems to become more complex in its manifestation, impacting on emotional well-being. Research by Skinner and Piek, for example, has demonstrated the mental impact of DCD, manifesting in lower self-worth, greater anxiety and weaker social support than non-DCD peers (even when the child is still at junior school) (Skinner and Piek 2001, p.73). This chapter (and the sections in Chapter Five on sleeplessness and obsessive thinking) contrast with Chapters Three and Four as the focus is on life outside the education system because, for the dyspraxic, the effects of dyspraxia are pervasive, affecting all aspects of life. However, although this chapter does not directly address the impact of the emotional effects of dyspraxia in the classroom, it is hoped that strategies covered will have a positive effect in the classroom too.

Where the role of the occupational therapist (OT) is of primary importance for physical dyspraxia, psychological support becomes increasingly important as the child gets older. Parents of infant school children are sometimes told that their child's dyspraxia has been cured or controlled for the future after a course of coordination exercises from an OT, leaving the child to move forward into adolescence coping alone with the emotional and social effects of dyspraxia. Although the OT is often the first source of assessment and remedial strategies, the psychiatrist or psychologist can play an invaluable role in providing coping strategies for the adolescent or adult dyspraxic.

The Dyspraxia Foundation website lists emotional difficulties associated with dyspraxia:

- sleep difficulties
- self-esteem issues and emotional volatility
- depression, stress and anxiety.

Many of these characteristics are not unique to people with dyspraxia and not even the most severe case will have all the above characteristics. But adults with dyspraxia will tend to have more than their fair share of co-ordination and perceptual difficulties.

(Dyspraxia Foundation 2014f)

The emotional consequences of dyspraxia may be partly neurological or genetic, but are also psychological, resulting from the difficulties caused by dyspraxia. For example, difficulties with social skills could be attributed to neurological immaturity, but are also clearly connected with the social experiences of the child with dyspraxia. Stress and anxiety could have a genetic basis, but are also psychological states of emotion. Emotional consequences of dyspraxia can lead to:

- emotional volatility
- low self-esteem
- anxious thoughts
- stress
- social difficulties.

Emotional challenges faced by adolescent dyspraxics can easily become allied to academic progress and may become barriers to:

- academic learning
- academic performance
- living a fully fulfilling life.

All of the emotional challenges faced by the learner with dyspraxia can result in a lack of fulfilment and wasted potential. Dyspraxic lives can be ruined if the mental consequences of dyspraxia are not addressed.

Emotional volatility

Although some of the emotional consequences of dyspraxia may have a neural base, it could also be that the frustration which dyspraxia causes, both physically and mentally, makes the sorely tried dyspraxic irritable, prone to rages and extremes of emotion. The mental and physical unpredictability of dyspraxia can represent for some an endless, emotional rollercoaster ride, leading to real anxiety and emotional volatility. The refusal of the body to cooperate and perform in a coordinated way can lead to frustration and anger. There might also be rage at a world that cannot be controlled, a world in which, at times, the person with dyspraxia can be labelled as 'useless' simply because of a lack of physical dexterity and prowess. Fluctuations of temperament can be extreme for some dyspraxics, whatever their age.

The two key states of emotional volatility which seem to be associated with dyspraxia are:

- overreacting
- irritability.

Both of these emotions can cause difficulty in an educational environment.

All the emotional states of dyspraxia are interconnected. Irritability may be caused by stress, frustration or anxiety so when, for example, stress is tackled successfully, a result could be reduced irritability.

Overreaction

Overreaction is caused by strength of emotions and results in impulsive behaviour and emotional extremes. This will manifest as being:

- easily upset
- hypersensitive
- negative
- over-dramatic
- argumentative.

And having:

- uncontrolled reactions, even to minor incidents
- instantaneous reactions without engaging in rational thought first
- a tendency to react instantly to any situation.

A tendency to overreact can be checked by:

- strategies from the *anxiety* and *stress* sections
- self-awareness – identifying the 'triggers' for overreaction
- a 'wait and see' procrastination approach – there are times when it is better to 'keep your head down' than to be a 'drama queen'
- remembering that for every negative, tricky dyspraxic day, there will be a good day when life moves forward more easily and situations are managed in a more straightforward way.

Irritability

Anger or irritability should not be 'bottled up' but controlled: there are times when irritation or anger is necessary but there are also situations socially and academically where anger needs to be controlled as a damage-limitation exercise. Colley advises dyspraxics to 'master impulsiveness and anger' (Colley 2006, p.51).

To contain irritability:

- Be accepting and observant of each day, whatever the mood – there will always be 'tetchy' days.

- Be observant of anger or irritation as it develops (see section on *repetitive thinking*).

- Try not to overreact to people or situations.

- Adopt a calm approach – this will achieve more than aggression. ('A soft answer turneth away wrath', Proverbs 15 v.1, *Revised English Bible* 1989)

(See also the section on *strategies for calm*, page 145.)

Low self-esteem

Dyspraxic people are not born with low self-esteem but the clumsy episodes, poor performance in physical activities and, at times, the impossibility of performing simple physical tasks can be demoralising. There must be a moment of acute self-awareness for the child with dyspraxia at school – the moment when they do something clumsy, when a chair is tripped over or a ball is not caught and the discomfort of this moment will be exacerbated during the school years by the presence of a fairly large audience to capture and maybe even to ridicule every physical mishap. By their teens, or even while still at junior school, it is almost inevitable that the child with dyspraxia will become increasingly self-conscious about their physicality and could easily begin to suffer from poor self-esteem and a lack of confidence. Unfortunately, these traits are not easily altered and seem to become more deeply entrenched, particularly in the teenage years.

Self-esteem will affect not only how a person thinks about themselves but also their interactions with other people and their perceptions of how others see them. These perceptions may be very negative or even inaccurate. The three main causes of lack of self-esteem for dyspraxics as they grow older are probably:

- lack of physical proficiency
- learning difficulties
- other people's reactions.

Bullying

In *Kaplan and Sadock's Concise Textbook of Child and Adolescent Psychiatry*, Benjamin and Virginia Sadock note the self-esteem issues which can develop for adolescents with coordination difficulties, referring also to the self-esteem issues which may result from bullying (Sadock and Sadock 2009, p.45). People in any environment and at any age will bully partly because they are uneasy with anyone who does not fit in to a social 'norm'. Unfortunately, children (and adults) will often follow the lead of the group which is ostracising an individual and the individual will, consequently, become more isolated and less confident of their social skills.

For dyspraxics, bullying can be particularly difficult to handle because words can literally fail them. It should not really be the dyspraxic's purpose at school to deal with verbal bullies or silent bullying, when there are so many other issues to be tackled in a classroom environment. They do, however, need strategies for dealing with bullies, such as 'walking away', avoidance or pre-planned verbal responses. The Dyspraxia Foundation has published two short guides on bullying:

- *Seeing Your Way Through: Beat the Bullies – A Guide for Children* (Dyspraxia Foundation (2013b))
- *Seeing Your Way Through: Bullying – A Guide for Parents* (Dyspraxia Foundation (2013c)).

Strategies for tackling low self-esteem

There is an arsenal of strategies, both physical and mental, which can be used to challenge lack of self-esteem and confidence issues. It would be irresponsible to claim that any strategy could completely eradicate the emotional challenges faced by students with dyspraxia, but practising and assimilating some of these strategies can make school, university and life generally, a little easier:

- visualisation techniques
- adopting someone else's skin
- posture

- experiment
- positive affirmations.

Visualisation techniques

A dyslexic neighbour once told me that she finds she can do things she does not think she is going to be able to do, if she visualises herself doing them successfully. Athletes often use this type of imagery, and according to sport psychologist David Yukelson of Penn State University, it can also be used as a coping skill, a communication tool or when learning a new task. Yukelson describes visualisation as creating a vivid, visual image, using emotions, senses and adrenaline, which should then strengthen neural pathways (Yukelson n.d. p.1).

Of course, this technique is not about eliminating the physical difficulties of dyspraxia, but it is about challenging the mindscapes that accompany it:

- Lack of self-esteem and self-confidence.
- Fear of being ridiculed for making a mistake.
- Reluctance to participate in group activities.
- Aversion to trying anything new, for fear of failing.
- Avoidance of social interaction.

By harnessing the ability that human beings have to change their thought patterns, visualisation techniques can be a valuable tool for challenging negative self-esteem and boosting self-confidence.

Adopting someone else's skin

American author Jonathan Safran Froer has to be the best example of assuming another identity to cope, at those anxious, stressful times when he is simply unable to be himself. When Jonathan Safran Froer was nine years old he was caught in an explosion in a chemistry lesson at summer camp. For the next three years he suffered from what he has described as a nervous breakdown. In an interview with Suzie Mackenzie, Froer explains that, when he was 12, he realised that his coping mechanism needed to be dissociation, and he achieves this by imagining himself to be someone who can cope with whatever situation he is dealing with. For example, as an adult he has become a writer and is expected to give readings. He suffers from stage fright, so when he has to speak in public, he simply pretends to be someone else (*The Guardian* 2005).

Posture

Most people are born with perfect posture. Until they are at infant school, children will sit in a perfectly natural position with a beautifully straight back, which is not forced into position. Most teenagers and adults seem to lose this perfect posture as they become more self-aware.

Writer and educator Mark Rowh refers to a 2009 study by Naumann *et al.* that cited clothing and posture as influencing first impressions (Rowh 2012, p.32).

As discussed in Chapter Two, there are various causes, both physical and mental, of poor posture for the dyspraxic, and these postural difficulties will have a physical impact in the classroom and an impact on how an individual is perceived by others. For the dyspraxic who is ill at ease with themselves, the effect on posture could, in fact, mean an endless reinforcement of negative self-image as a result of the reactions of others. And these 'others' are, of course, not responding to the dyspraxic as an individual but to the self-image that is portrayed in their posture.

Health psychologist Kelly McGonigal discusses the effect of posture on self-esteem in *Psychology Today*, referring to research into the influence of posture on self-confidence. According to McGonical, Brion, Petty and Wagner found that if a mock job application form was completed while slumped in a chair, the mock-applicant would be less confident of their suitability for the job, than the applicants who filled in the form while sitting confidently, with good posture (McGonigal 2009).

Walking tall not only improves confidence but also improves the image that is presented to other people. Alexander Technique taught me to focus on having a long neck when walking. This particular technique is a 'quick fix' for poor posture because by focusing on the head and neck, better posture occurs automatically, without any strained attempts to achieve good posture through a straight back (see also Chapter Two).

Experiment

Even the basic things which are learned in life, for example tying a shoelace or telling the time, may take longer to learn for someone with dyspraxia because of a lack of physical dexterity or slower automaticity for learning new tasks. It is particularly easy for the dyspraxic to stop trying to learn new skills and activities as a result of negative learning experiences in the past, when at times they might have wondered whether a skill could ever be acquired. It may take longer to learn something new but once a skill or activity has been learned, the dyspraxic person will be just as adept as anyone else. Practice and developing new skills are subtly connected with self-esteem. This is why it is particularly important for the dyspraxic to accept a challenge, to experiment and to persevere with new activities.

(See also the section on *practice* in Chapter Two, page 44.)

Positive affirmations

For the dyspraxic, the ability to learn and to succeed at different skills and activities needs to be anchored in their thoughts because without the acknowledgement that they can persevere and achieve, many dyspraxics will simply 'give up' the will to learn or to try new things. To anchor self-image, a mental checklist of physical achievements and cognitive aptitudes could be used to counteract negative feelings about physical difficulties and areas of mental weakness.

(See also the section on *anchors* on page 143.)

Anxious thoughts

(See also 'hazard warning sign' in the *sleeplessness* section of Chapter Five, page 125.)

Dyspraxia manifests in such a maelstrom of different ways, both mentally and physically, that it is almost inevitable that the dyspraxic individual will be an anxious individual. Research into anxiety and behavioural difficulties in children diagnosed with DCD, by Michelle Pratt and Elizabeth Hill, has supported the findings of earlier researchers, that children with DCD develop high anxiety and emotional issues (Pratt and Hill 2010).

Strategies for coping with anxious thoughts

As with all the traits associated with the dyspraxic mind, there is an arsenal of weapons which can be used to combat anxiety. Of course, anxious tendencies cannot be cured, but strategies for controlling anxiety can be adopted. Dyspraxia plays unwitting mind games on the individual, so mind games can be played to combat the dyspraxia:

- worry later
- double think

- anchors
- CBT techniques
- brain space.

(See also *engaging the senses* in the section on stress, on page 145.)

Worry later

Eckhart Tolle quotes the Indian philosopher Krishnamurti, whose secret was this: 'I don't mind what happens' (Tolle 2009, p.198). Anxiety and worry tend to be about what will happen in the future, rather than what is happening at this moment. Author Oliver Burkeman writes (with reference to the ideas of leading psychotherapist Albert Ellis), '"What's the worst that could happen?" The answer is sometimes pretty bad. But it is finitely bad, rather than infinitely terrifying, so there is always a chance of coping with it' (Burkeman 2012, p.210).

An effective tool for controlling anxiety is to defer the worry until later, simply by thinking, 'I will worry about that later.' Eckhart Tolle writes:

> Ask yourself what problem you have right now, not next year, tomorrow, or five minutes from now. What is wrong with the moment? You can always cope with the Now, but you can never cope with the future – nor do you have to. The answer, the strength, the right action or the resource will be there when you need it, not before, not after. (Tolle 2005, p.70)

Double think

Anxious or negative, repetitive thoughts can be controlled by examining them in a more objective, less subjective way by asking the following questions:

- Is there a different or more positive perspective on the situation?
- Are there more positive outcomes than the one I am dwelling on?
- What is the worst-case scenario and how would I cope?

Anchors

Anchors are a useful tool, often used in Neuro-Linguistic Programming (Bandler and Grinder 1979). This method can be useful to store positive memories to refer to when anxiety occurs. Anchoring is:

A process of associating an internal response (a desirable emotion) with some internal or external trigger so that the response may be quickly, and often covertly, reaccessed... [Like ships] we can choose where we want to keep ourselves to avoid drifting into feelings of tension, stress or worry, for example. (Knight 2010, p.169)

Here are some examples of anchors which can be used to challenge preconceived worries:

Anxious thought	Anchor
Agitation about another person's behaviour or something they have said.	Remember something positive about that person – something they have said or done or even a mannerism.
Fear of a future event.	Focus on an event or situation which caused unnecessary apprehension.
Fear of change.	Anchor to any positive changes that have been made, for example changes of job or relocation.

(See also *positive affirmations* in the section on low self-esteem, on page 142.)

Cognitive Behavioural Therapy (CBT) techniques

Cognitive behavioural therapist Dr Robert Leahy listed the following CBT techniques for taming anxiety, during an interview with Jon Ronson:

- Confront fears by 'hoping' that the worry will happen. ['I hope that I fail my exams!']

- Recognise the difference between different types of worry: the worries that can be solved and those that cannot be solved.

- Repeat the unresolvable worry until the mind becomes bored with it and moves on to something else.

- Live in the present; don't worry about the future.

(*The Guardian* 2013a)

Brain space

Sunny Jacobs, who spent more than 15 years in solitary confinement on death row for a crime she had not committed, decided that she could be imprisoned physically, but her mind remained her own space, which no one else could control (*The Guardian* 2013b). Ultimately, every individual has some control over their brain and the thoughts that present and the effect that they have. Basically, humans are neurological machines and machines are operable.

Sensory strategies can also be useful at times of anxiety. (See the *stress strategies* section on *engaging the senses* below.)

Stress: strategies for calm

It is almost inevitable that the complex difficulties associated with dyspraxia will result in stress, even for the mildly dyspraxic person. Here are some strategies that can be used to ease stress:

- engaging the senses
- breathing
- mindfulness
- meditation.

Engaging the senses

Another strategy for dealing with the mind games dyspraxia plays is simply to learn to focus on everything that is going on outside the conscious mind, with its endless stream of egotistical thinking, by concentrating on the five senses and what is being experienced in the present. The senses can be used as an instant and easy calming tactic, for example:

- Focusing on what can be seen, heard, touched and smelled in the immediate moment.
- 'Thinking big' by being aware of the infinite space beyond the individual self, and its physical and mental constraints.
- An Alexander Technique exercise encourages the individual to focus intention on, for example, the arm, thinking oneself outside of the physical self.
- Square exercise: find something square to look at, for example a picture. Keep visually tracking the square shape, round and round.

All of the strategies listed above could be described as 'distraction' techniques.

Breathing

There are many different breathing strategies which can be used to reduce stress and induce relaxation generally, and these techniques can be particularly useful just before:

- examinations
- interviews
- presentations.

Various breathing strategies

There are various calming, breathing techniques which can be useful for combating stress:

- 555. Breathe in to the count of five, hold for the count of five, out for the count of five.
- 7:11. Breathe in to the count of seven, out to the count of eleven.
- Count down from 100 in sevens. The mind can only really concentrate on one thing at a time and the mental calculation involved in counting down acts as a useful calming, distractive tool.
- To relax just before any stressful situation, for example before an interview, before public speaking or even just before entering a room full of doting relatives: 'Breathe in for three counts; hold breath for three counts; breathe out for three counts. Repeat, increasing the counts' (Marash 1947, p.35).

(See also breathing strategies in the section on *sleeplessness* in Chapter Five, page 123.)

Deep breathing technique

Deep or belly breathing techniques can be particularly useful for tackling stress. It is important, with deep breathing, to focus on breathing out fully and then to relax and allow the in-breath to flow in from the belly upwards. If the in-breath is taken actively and taken in the upper chest this can trigger the 'fight or flight' mode, the result being a state of permanent adrenaline-induced stress! Voice-coaching expert Barbara Houseman taught me to breathe through the diaphragm using this deep breathing technique:

- Place one hand on the stomach and the other hand lightly on the chest bone.

- Breathe normally and notice movement of the hands.
- Ideally the movement should start in the belly and move gently up towards the chest as if the lungs are filling from their base and are doing so deep inside the body.
- To help this happen, breathe out fully as if sighing with contentment or relief and let the belly fall in towards the spine, while the chest gently melts rather than sharply drops.
- Relax the belly and let the breath fill up from the bottom again.
- This process is about taking the breath fully into the lungs, rather than simply into the top of the lungs.

This technique is the best I have ever known for de-stressing, and the simplest, harnessing something everyone has to do, every minute of our lives. It takes practice though, and if in doubt about how to do it properly, ask a voice expert.

Mindfulness

Recent research has found that mindfulness-based therapy is particularly useful for reducing stress, anxiety and depression (Khoury *et al.* 2013). In January 2012, as something of a New Year sweetener, BBC Breakfast promoted mindfulness meditation and the effect it can have on positive thinking and the reduction of stress and anxiety. When scanned by neuroscientists, Buddhist monk Matthieu Ricard's brain was found to have a high level of activity in the part of his brain associated with positivity (Sillito 2012). Ricard is an expert in meditative practice, so his brain scan is evidence that meditation really is good for the mind.

Mindfulness tends to focus on the physical, including breathing. As the thoughts pass through the mind during mindfulness practice, each thought, although noted, is simply not pursued. The aim is to be:

- more observant
- less self-absorbed
- more detached from stressful, negative or anxious thoughts.

Mindfulness is a flexible technique for reducing stress, which can be practised:

- anywhere
- anytime
- sitting or walking.

Mindfulness can be practised fleetingly, for example while walking along a corridor or waiting for a lesson or lecture. Or it can be practised for longer, with a 10- or 20-minute session at the beginning or end of each day.

Meditation practitioner Eric Harrison of the Perth Meditation Centre writes that meditation or mindfulness involves two skills, based simultaneously on relaxation and attention:

- 'learning how to relax quickly and consciously'

- '"thought control" or paying attention…becoming able to direct our thoughts, to switch thoughts and abandon thoughts, and to wind back mental activity at will.'

(Harrison n.d.)

The result is physical relaxation and mental calmness. And it is that focus on the physical and on the mental that makes mindfulness so well suited to individuals with dyspraxia.

Three-minute meditation

An informal, three-minute mindfulness meditation can be done anywhere, at any time of day. Psychologist and director of Oxford University's Mindfulness Centre Professor Mark Williams has a brief video guide to a three-minute meditation (Williams 2014). In brief, the technique for Williams's *three minute breathing space* is:

Step 1

- Focus on the present moment:
    - thoughts
    - emotions
    - feelings in body.
- Accept thoughts, emotions and feelings as they are in the present moment.

Step 2

- Focus on the sensation of the in-breath and the out-breath.
- Guide the mind back to the breath if it wanders away.

Step 3

- Expand awareness to body as a breathing whole and to sensations in the body.

- Accept things as they are. Be open to the moment and what is here, now.

Ten-minute mindfulness meditation

As part of the BBC Breakfast Happiness Challenge in January 2011, Andy Puddicombe of HeadSpace demonstrated a ten-minute mindfulness exercise, which can be found at www.bbc.co.uk/news/12263893 (Sillito 2011).

Mindfulness visualisation

Visualisation can also be used as part of a longer mindfulness meditation, for example imagine walking towards a favourite place and sitting down to enjoy it, while still breathing slowly.

An example of a visual mindfulness meditation is Jon Kabat-Zinn's *Lake Meditation*:

- Visualise a lake at different times of the day and in different weather.

- Imagine being the lake in its entirety with its changing flow.

(Kabat-Zinn 2004, p.141)

Visualisation can be tacked onto the three-minute mindfulness meditation.

Mindfulness-based Cognitive Therapy (MBCT)

Mindfulness-based Cognitive Therapy (MBCT) was developed by John Teasdale, Zindel Segal and Mark Williams, originating from Jon Kabat-Zinn's Mindfulness-based Stress Reduction programme. Williams went on to develop an eight-week MBCT course, which is used by the NHS. For details and guidance on this eight-week programme, see Mark Williams and Danny Penman's book, *Mindfulness: a practical guide to finding peace in a frantic world* (Williams and Penman 2011).

Social difficulties

Social effects

The social difficulties associated with dyspraxia should not be underestimated, and will have an impact on other areas of life. These difficulties can be exacerbated early in life, at a stage when physical performance in the playground and on the playing field is so very important socially. *Kaplan and Sadock's Concise Textbook of Child and Adolescent Psychiatry* mentions the difficulties that individuals with DCD have in social relationships with peers, resulting from lack of sporting prowess (Sadock and Sadock 2009, p.45).

'Difference' is fundamental to social difficulties for the dyspraxic. It is inevitable that dyspraxia will result in a level of non-conformity because the dyspraxic person is physically and mentally 'different'. Most dyspraxics will have friends and a social life but may be less comfortable in large groups. Also, the more 'conformist' or traditional the environment, the more likely it is that social rejection might occur for the non-conformist dyspraxic, and the more acutely aware of social difficulties they will become. If social experiences have been awkward at school, then these experiences are likely to be repeated later on. Unfortunately, children (and adults) will follow the lead of the group which is ostracising an individual and the individual will become more isolated and less confident of their social skills. Possibly, for student dyspraxics in tertiary education, it is easier to escape overt labels such as 'clumsy' and to have access to a broader catchment of friends than they would within the confines of a community school. (See also the *bullying* section earlier in this chapter, page 139.)

Social difficulties could result from neurological immaturities, as well as the emotional consequences of other people's reactions and behaviour. According to teacher and author Geoff Brookes, dyspraxics will 'struggle to pick up non-verbal signals or misread the tone of others. They might take things too literally' (Brookes 2007, p.109). Auditory processing difficulties and tactile sensitivity might also affect social interaction. Effects of dyspraxia on social skills might include:

- inclination to interrupt
- impulsiveness
- oversensitivity
- self-consciousness
- being over-emotional
- shyness
- being easily offended, resulting in 'dropping' friends
- distractibility
- sensitivity to physical proximity and contact
- tactlessness.

There might also be difficulties with:

- recognising social cues

- comprehending facial expressions
- controlling own body language
- understanding body language of others
- eye contact
- conversation
- listening
- discriminating between friendship and polite disengagement.

Other people's social reactions are not, however, necessarily personal. Sharon Sayler writes that dislike of others can result from reactions to body language cues (Sayler 2010). These reactions are innate and, therefore, dislike is not necessarily based on personality or conviviality. For people with dyspraxia, appropriate body language and eye contact cues can be difficult to understand, and this can be a further factor contributing to social difficulties. Innate social difficulties could also become more dominant as a result of negative social experiences, and the outcome could be that the dyspraxic might become nervous around other people. This could lead to fickleness in friendships, a lack of trust and difficulties in establishing strong friendships. Geoff Brookes acknowledges that for the dyspraxic, 'Uncertainty in relationships with their peers can mean that they are not sure how genuine others are, so isolation and loneliness can be inevitable' (Brookes 2007, p.110).

It is worth noting that an important social strength is strongly associated with dyspraxia, and that is the ability to be hugely empathic and sensitive to other people. Possibly, an awareness of others is heightened by the difficulties caused by dyspraxia. This means that in the right context, others may seek the dyspraxic out for their empathy, creating an instinctive social connection.

Social burden

Dyspraxia carries something of a social burden because the dyspraxic does not necessarily want to be isolated and is likely to be sociable, but may lack the skills to socialise. An anonymous person with Asperger syndrome writes that they like people, desperately want to have friends and a partner, to be able to make conversation and to socialise, but quite simply cannot accomplish these things. This person's anguish is heartfelt and they argue that, for humans, the ability to interact socially is a basic need (*The Guardian* 2011a).

Social skills strategies

People are not mindreaders, so nerves and anxieties can remain invisible, hidden behind social strategies. There are many strategies which can be used to compensate for or tackle social difficulties:

- first impressions
- eye contact
- conversation:
  - timing
  - interrupting
  - different methods of conversing
  - asking questions
  - listening.
- focusing outwards:
  - cameras out
  - alternative realities.
- familiar strangers.

For social situations, key strategies to ease communication and reduce stress or anxiety include:

- deep breathing
- focusing outwards
- listening.

First impressions

(See also the section on *posture* earlier in this chapter, page 141.)

First impressions are made in three to five seconds (Quast 2013) and will influence future social interactions or success at interviews. First impressions are based on:

- eye contact
- voice tone
- attire and grooming
- confidence of body language.

The key components of first impressions are all things that can be subject to individual control. All of these things can be changed. Social psychologist Amy Cuddy has researched the premise 'Can you fake it until you make it?' and has found evidence that assuming a confident body pose can actually result in greater confidence, leading her to conclude that it is, in fact, possible to 'fake it till you become it' (Cuddy 2012).

Eye contact

People with dyspraxia may avoid eye contact or have difficulty gauging how much eye contact is needed. Perhaps eye contact feels too personal or intrusive, or a heightened neuro-sensitivity makes this type of unspoken communication difficult. Eye contact is important because it enables engagement, communication and connection with other people but it needs to be carefully balanced because too much eye contact can be unnerving and too little can suggest lack of confidence.

Ben Decker of San Francisco-based Decker Communications writes that:

> Recently, someone came into my office with eyes darting all around – left, right, up and down. This person displayed a lack of confidence. And what's worse, it looked shifty, unsure, and a bit jittery. When I saw this, I translated it into a lack of trust for this individual. I couldn't help it – nor can you…it's an instinct, a feeling… Hold your gaze. (Decker 2014)

This demonstrates the importance of eye contact and how lack of eye contact can result in misconceptions and affect an individual's credibility. It is unfortunate that preliminary personal judgements are made on eye contact, rather than personalities, but humans are conditioned to make quick judgements about strangers.

For the dyspraxic, there could well be something slightly insincere or contrived about controlling eye contact, but eye contact is a crucial component of social interaction, so it could be very useful to practise different strategies for it. For one-to-one conversations, the eye contact triangle could be a useful tool for a dyspraxic who is uncomfortable with maintaining eye contact. Instead of making direct eye contact, focus on a triangular facial area, around the eyes. This gives the illusion of eye contact. Sharon Sayler describes two types of triangle:

- a triangle between the eyes and the forehead.

- an inverted triangle between the eyebrows and the nose.

According to Sayler, the first triangle is more appropriate for communication in formal situations, while the second triangle is appropriate for social communication (Sayler 2010).

Other strategies that can be used are:

- When talking, maintain eye contact to engage the listener, but glance away briefly to gather thoughts or words.

- When listening, maintain eye contact to show engagement, but glance away to visualise what is being heard.

- While briefly breaking eye contact, focus can be retained by looking at the conversant's face, using the eye triangle.

Eye contact is a prerequisite not only of one-to-one talking and listening, but also of group communication. For group eye contact tactics, Kelly Vandever, president of Communications for Everyone, recommends gauging eye contact changes by stating a thought or finishing a sentence, before moving eye contact to someone else in the group (Vandever 2014).

Conversation

Conversation is a particularly complicated social skill and for some dyspraxics who have difficulty in planning and sequencing thoughts, and associated difficulties with verbalising those thoughts, conversation and 'small talk' can be challenging. It is ironic that dyspraxics who are oversensitive about what is said to them spend a lot of time being tactless through sheer awkwardness and an inability to think coherently from moment to moment, and thus agonise afterwards not only about what has been said to them but about what they have said to others!

In awkward social situations it should be helpful to remain:

- calm

- still

- focused

- aware of conversational cues and follow them.

And to remember to:

- acknowledge that others are equally responsible for the conversation

- allow other people to talk

- let other people prompt the conversation.

Some types of conversation are more difficult than others. The type of unforced chatter which occurs naturally in, for example, a classroom can be more straightforward than a chance encounter in the street, where it is easy to say the wrong thing or use the wrong phraseology, or a classroom question from a teacher when the mind might quite simply fail to remember the right response. West distinguishes between 'demand language' (where a response is required and because thoughts are elsewhere the verbal response required socially cannot be mustered) and 'spontaneous' language, which can be less complicated because the speaker is taking the initiative (West 1991, p.182).

Interrupting

One of the key weaknesses which some dyspraxics bring to social situations is a capacity for interrupting. This could stem from:

- concentration issues
- an inability to recognise the cues that another person has finished speaking
- auditory issues.

Dyspraxic champion Mary Colley writes that:

Sometimes we wait for the other speaker to draw breath and then blurt out ideas we have not thought through. The way that we communicate can be negative, competitive and self-centred. Our tendency to interrupt and the lack of reciprocity can be frustrating for family, friends and colleagues. (Colley 2006, p.49)

Timing

For the dyspraxic, closely connected with interrupting is difficulty in judging timing of a conversation. Appropriate timing can make a significant difference to outcome. Mary Colley advises that, 'Choosing the right time and place to bring up a topic can make all the difference between being listened to and being ignored' (Colley 2006, p.51).

Different types of conversation

Dr Scott Williams from Wright State University, Ohio, writes that the most common mistaken conversational response is 'to give advice or deflect in a situation where counseling is appropriate' (Williams n.d.).The conversational trait of deflection moves the conversation to another topic. Williams suggests that deflection needs to be used carefully because deflection 'can unintentionally communicate that we haven't listened and that we aren't interested… Many of us deflect unwittingly by sharing our personal experiences when we should be focusing on the other party' (Williams n.d.).

According to Williams, a counselling response requires two conversational tools:

- Reflecting – 'paraphrasing back to the speaker what they said', which also acts as a conversational lead because questions can be asked.

- Probing – non-judgementally asking for additional information about what has just been said.

(Williams n.d.)

These two techniques are taught to trainee Citizen's Advice Bureau advisers because often the client's meaning is subject to misinterpretation and might require clarification.

Asking questions

Questions can be asked to move the conversation forward but should not rely on intrusive personal questions. Colley encourages adults with dyspraxia to be aware that personal questions or comments can cause embarrassment or make others feel uncomfortable (Colley 2006, p.51). If questions are not too probing and follow conversational leads, then the conversant will engage. Most people like to talk about themselves.

Listening

According to listening expert Dr Ralph Nichols, 'The most basic of all human needs is the need to understand and be understood. The best way to understand people is to listen to them' (Nichols 1980, p.5). Lack of concentration is not just limited to the classroom and, of course, can occur socially as well. In social situations, there can be a tendency for the dyspraxic person to:

- lack concentration
- be easily distracted
- interrupt

- speak impulsively
- fail to speak at all.

Listening is good for calming nerves and for social interaction. The anxious thoughts which so often seem to be present in the dyspraxic mind can become so preoccupying that it is difficult to listen not only to random small talk but also to the people who really matter, to family and friends. Listening requires:

- presence
- patience
- concentration
- eye contact
- non-verbal cues, e.g. nodding
- awareness of the speaker's non-verbal cues, e.g. hand gestures, voice pitch and tone
- empathy
- non-judgemental attitude.

Listening skills do not just require silence though. A good listener will respond verbally too, through paraphrasing and questions, but without interrupting or deflecting.

Focusing outwards

(See also the section on *self-esteem*, page 138.)

Dyspraxia can be a very introspective condition. People who have grown up with dyspraxia tend to feel physically self-conscious, possibly because even the simplest physical tasks have been so difficult at times, and other people, particularly during the school years, have subjected them to so much critical scrutiny. These experiences can lead to self-conscious feelings of physical gawkiness or awkwardness when speaking. A friend of author Maeve Binchy's mother gave her some useful advice: people are too preoccupied with looking at themselves to look at anyone else; no one looks at anyone else (*The Guardian* 1985).

In the Pont cartoon, *Popular Misconceptions – the People Behind* (Laidler 1942, p.61), the people in the pews behind a small boy at a church service have horns, monstrous moustaches and outrageous hats. For the dyspraxic, this is how strangers can seem, possibly partly as a result of unpleasant experiences of other people at school, which can lead at times to a real reluctance to engage with others at all. In social situations, it can help simply to observe that other people are not monsters at all, they are just other human beings, each with their own human frailties. Two strategies which can be used to counterbalance self-consciousness and social stress are:

- Barbara Houseman's *Cameras out* acting technique.
- Robert Leahy's *Alternative realities* cognitive behavioural technique.

Cameras out

A useful technique for focusing outwards in social situations is *Cameras out* (Houseman 2008, pp18–20). This technique was devised by the voice coach and acting director Barbara Houseman, and it aims to tackle self-consciousness by encouraging a non-judgemental focus on other people. This technique allows focus to move away from the self to observe instead other people's:

- clothing
- facial features
- body language
- mood
- nervousness
- physical awkwardness
- conversation
- sound of voice.

It can be helpful when using *Cameras out* to observe that social stress is not solely a dyspraxic trait and that other people feel uncomfortable or awkward socially, and other people have clumsy moments too. Everyone has good moments and bad moments, good days and bad days, dyspraxic moments and non-dyspraxic moments.

Alternative realities

Cognitive therapist Dr Robert Leahy's advice for dealing with social anxiety is to observe and be aware that everyone at a social event has their own 'reality' which gives them an individual perspective and their responses to others relate to themselves and their reactions, not their reaction to the other person. He recommends seeing a party from the viewpoint of five other guests (Leahy 2006).

Familiar strangers

Finally, it is useful to recognise that social difficulties are part of the human condition, not limited solely to people with dyspraxia. Many people suffer from social awkwardness and anxiety. The concept of the 'familiar stranger' could be of value to anyone who is hypersensitive about their relationships with others because it shows how uncomfortable people are socially with strangers. Stanley Milgram studied 'familiar strangers' in the 1970s, researching New York commuters to try to understand the role of unspeaking strangers who share a station platform every day of their working lives. He found that it becomes increasingly difficult for familiar strangers to talk, but if they see each other in a different context, for example, on holiday, they will talk as if they are acquainted (Paulos and Goodman 2004, p.1).

It is not just strangers who ignore each other. An anonymous teenager asks why we ignore friends or schoolmates who have not been seen for a while. And the answers are:

- fear of being ignored
- not being 'mentally prepared'
- not 'looking at best'
- feeling guilty about not speaking afterwards
- shyness
- people change and become more like strangers.

(Yahoo! Answers 2007)

These answers also show that social anxiety happens to everyone, not just those within the narrower definition of dyspraxia.

(To tackle oversensitivity see strategies for dealing with *repetitive thinking* in Chapter Five, page 131.)

CHAPTER SEVEN
PREPARING FOR WORK

Although the overall aim of this book is to suggest strategies which can be useful for learners with dyspraxia at secondary school, college and university, it also aims to provide strategies for teenagers and young adults moving from education into the workplace. The child with dyspraxia experiencing difficulties in the classroom can quite easily go on to experience difficulties in the workplace and these difficulties will remain both physically and mentally diverse. Equally, dyspraxia can bring key strengths to working life, and to employers. *Working with Dyspraxia: a hidden asset*, a Dyspraxia Foundation guide for employers, refers to the qualities which dyspraxia brings to the workplace, 'Persistence, determination and extremely hard working are all characteristics associated with dyspraxia – which makes people with this condition valuable employees' (Dyspraxia Foundation 2012a, p.3).

This chapter will discuss:

- workplace difficulties
- workplace strengths
- strategies for the workplace
- employer strategies for the workplace
- employee strategies for the workplace
- proactive employers
- careers
- interview techniques
- presentation techniques
- learning to drive.

The Disability Discrimination Act 1995 (DDA) states that employers and education providers are not allowed to discriminate against employees or learners with disablties. The Equality Act 2010 legislates for reasonable adjustments to be made for people with disablties in the workplace. A reasonable adjustment should take into account physical difficulties and working differences experienced by any employee who declares an SpLD or a physical difficulty. Trade unions are there to challenge discriminatory practices in the workplace and will seek to ensure that adjustments are made for workers with disabilities.

Workplace difficulties

Difficulties which people with dyspraxia may experience in the workplace are:

- Postural discomfort when sitting at a desk for long periods.
- Muscle and joint problems leading to back, wrist and arm pain when working at a computer or lifting.
- Poor spatial awareness and coordination difficulties that can lead to:
  - difficulties in operating machinery and equipment
  - clumsiness and trips, bumps and even falls
  - difficulties involving fine motor skills when using office equipment.
- Visual and auditory processing deficits that can lead to difficulties with:
  - reading and writing
  - sequencing
  - noise
  - bright office lighting
  - communication.
- Problems with planning and organisation.
- Poor time management.
- Weaknesses in concentration leading to errors in repetitive clerical tasks.
- Memory deficits that can lead to slower processing and automaticity when learning new skills, and a poor sense of direction.

All of the above have emotional consequences for the workplace dyspraxic, affecting:

- self-esteem

- social communication

- stress and anxiety.

Workplace strengths

Although the worker with dyspraxia can experience difficulties, these may be offset, at least partially, by a combination of cognitive strengths (see also Chapter One), such as:

- lateral thinking skills

- inventiveness

- attention to detail

- strategic thinking

- problem solving.

The worker with dyspraxia may also possess the following attributes:

- determination

- motivation

- creativity

- empathy.

Strategies for the workplace

The Government offers access to work funding that can be used for workplace adjustments and to ensure that employment is accessible. Examples of uses for this funding are:

- equipment modifications

- specialist equipment

- travel fares for employment

- relocation expenses

- support services or job coaches

- training on disability issues for colleagues.

(Gov.uk 2014)

Employer strategies for the workplace

Health and safety

Employers can make the following adjustments for workers with dyspraxia:

- adapted keyboard
- wrist rest
- foot rest
- manuscript stand
- ergonomic office chair
- appropriate desk
- left-handed scissors
- long-handled stapler
- regular breaks
- needs assessment for lifting.

The Health and Safety (Display Screen Equipment) Regulations 1992 require employers to undertake workstation assessments. This type of assessment can ensure that the workspace, including the desk area, is suitable for dyspraxic physical needs and can be carried out to identify necessary adjustments.

Dyspraxia awareness

It is particularly helpful if employers are aware of the dyspraxic profile and the contribution it can make to the workplace:

- Although employees with dyspraxia are slower to process new tasks, once a task has been mastered, the employee may be very competent.
- People with dyspraxia think differently and may bring new ideas and approaches into a business.
- Employees with dyspraxia tend to be hard-working and dependable.

Visual and auditory processing difficulties

Employers can help with visual and auditory processing difficulties by supplying:

- anti-glare screen filter
- cream-coloured paper
- reading and writing software
- a digital recorder
- coloured overlays.

Employee strategies for the workplace

Strategies for employees to try in the workplace:

- Record or write down instructions/procedures. Also, repeat them back at the moment they are given, to reinforce them sequentially.
- Video-record new procedures/tasks on a mobile phone.
- To enable concentration, wear earplugs or, conversely, listen to music through headphones.
- Use a stackable tray with an 'in' and a 'pending' tray to organise and prioritise work.
- Use a desktop planner, wall chart or computer planner/calendar to try to organise tasks and allocate adequate time and priority for each task.
- File regularly and carefully, with regard to alphabetical sequencing.
- Ask for help.

Lastly, never be afraid to ask for an accommodation to be made. Employers are not being malicious when they do not make adjustments or seem to be inept in their approach to health and safety; they simply do not always 'think'. I once worked at a college where I had to sit on a dining chair at a picnic/card table but as soon as this issue was raised, a suitable desk and office chair were produced immediately and the situation was rectified. In my experience, employers want to get the health and safety right because the last thing they want is injured or sick employees.

Disclosure

Skill (the National Bureau for Students with Disabilities) addresses educational and workplace disclosure in a useful leaflet, which gives information about disability legislation, the pros and cons of disclosure, and timing of disclosure. Ultimately, 'there is no clear-cut answer as to whether you should tell a prospective employer or institution that you are disabled. You must use your own judgement' (Skill 2005, p.1). For an example of a disclosure document, see the Dyspraxia Foundation's Dynamo Project (Dyspraxia Foundation 2012b).

See also Chapter Six for help with social and emotional effects of dyspraxia, because these factors will surely impact on the workplace experience given that such a sizeable portion of life may be spent there.

Proactive employers

Some employers already recognise the benefits that a neurodiverse profile can bring to business and so actively recruit dyspraxic and autistic staff. For example, the Civil Service has a proactive approach to neurological diversity and has developed a *Dyslexia and Dyspraxia Toolkit* for working with neurologically diverse employees. The Civil Service encourages managers to be aware of the following factors when working with employees with dyslexia or dyspraxia:

- Learning and activities may take longer
- Method may not be as important as results
- Recognition should be given to lateral thinking, which is associated with dyspraxia and dyslexia.

(Todd 2011, p.31)

In a speech on GCHQ and Turing's Legacy at the University of Leeds on 4 October 2012, Iain Lobban, Director of GCHQ, acknowledged the value of a diverse, non-stereotypical profile for innovative work such as code breaking, commenting that an intelligence agency cannot thrive if it does not recruit people who do not conform to social stereotypes (Lobban 2012). In an extract from an unpublished Equality and Human Rights Commission report, GCHQ also recognises the work it has done to help 'managers understand the amazing abilities that go with these "disabilities" and get real business to benefit from them' (Equality and Human Rights Commission 2009). When even one high-profile employer begins to respond to dyspraxia in this way, this recognition slowly infiltrates the workplace and the outlook for dyspraxia in the workplace, in the future, is promising.

Careers

It is hoped that employers are beginning to recognise that although dyspraxic employees can be slow to learn, once a task has been grasped they often perform it with extreme proficiency. How many dyspraxics have lost a job because the employer did not allow them the time to learn to do the job properly? Key dyspraxic cognitive characteristics could result in an aptitude for innovative, strategic or creative roles. Possibly, as a result of concentration or memory difficulties, some dyspraxics might be less well suited to repetitive, mundane tasks. Interestingly, according to Disability Salford, 'Many adults who have dyspraxia have careers in the caring or teaching profession and those who facilitate support groups are community workers' (Disability Salford n.d.).

Interview techniques

'At interview dyspraxia can affect many factors; speed of response to questions, ease of maintaining eye contact, speech, appearance which can be misinterpreted if the interviewer is not made aware of the profile' (Dyspraxia Foundation 2012a, p.9).

Pre-interview

Pre-interview strategies are particularly crucial for dyspraxic interview candidates, where planning and organisation can be so difficult. Advance planning needs to involve the following actions:

- Take dress code into consideration.
- Plan journey.
- Conduct research into employer.
- Thoroughly re-read the job description, in case any aspects of the job have been misunderstood.
- Ensure qualifications and skills or hobbies mentioned on the CV are committed to memory.
- Get a proper night's sleep. (See the section on *sleeplessness* in Chapter Five, page 123.)

It can also be useful to be prepared for interview questions and topics for discussion in advance:

- Think about strengths and weaknesses which will be brought to the job. These are standard questions, and the 'weaknesses' question requires a positive spin.

- Another standard question to prepare for is, 'Where would you like your career to progress to in five years' time?'

- If dyspraxia has been disclosed prior to the interview, be ready to discuss it in terms of adjustments the employer may need to make.

- Be aware in advance of questions which the interviewee might want to ask the employer.

Interview

Strategies to use during the interview:

- Turn mobile phone off.

- Pause for a moment to think and gather thoughts before answering a question.

- Do not lie or tell half-truths. Be straightforward in answering questions. Employers prefer this.

- Be positive. Focus on strengths which can be brought to the job and why the job is desirable.

(See Chapter Six for sections on *eye contact* (page 153) and *breathing techniques* (page 146), and below for *presentation techniques*.)

Panel-based interviews may have one member of the panel who is more sympathetic and another who is more aggressive towards the interview candidate. This can be difficult for a sensitive dyspraxic. It is really important to be aware that these are roles the interview panel assume to test the candidate. It is best not to react aggressively or defensively if one member of the panel is being aggressive, and also not to feel anger about this afterwards or to dwell on it. The employer is simply using this technique as part of the process of finding out which candidate will be the best one for the job.

The National Careers Service can offer interview and careers advice on the internet, by phone or by email, or through interviews with a local careers adviser. It can be found at https://nationalcareersservice.direct. gov.uk/Pages/Home.aspx.

Presentation techniques

For the learner with dyspraxia or employee, presentations can be particularly difficult not only because of anxiety and nervousness, but also because of difficulties in processing thoughts verbally. It is worth remembering that many people are uncomfortable about public speaking. Preparation in advance and breathing strategies are the two most useful strategies for presentations. The best strategy I know for nerves, taught to me by voice coach Barbara Houseman (and tried and tested by university students I have worked with), is deep breathing. (See Chapter Six for *deep breathing technique*, page 146.)

Preparation

Preparation is key to a nerveless delivery.

- Research the topic thoroughly.
- Engage with the subject.
- Be aware of the target audience's prior knowledge and what they will want to learn from the presentation.
- Put key points on index cards to take into the presentation.
- REHEARSE, REHEARSE, REHEARSE, preferably with an audience of at least one family member or a friend. A thorough advance knowledge of the talk is extremely useful for achieving calm delivery in the actual presentation. Rehearsing is also the only way to accurately test the length of the presentation.
- Record rehearsed speech, to reinforce it and gain familiarity with how it will sound to the audience.
- Try to be familiar with the room where the speech will be given.
- Visualise yourself in advance, giving your best possible speech – confident, knowledgeable and with an appreciative audience.

Delivery

- Have a drink of water available.
- Try to accept the nervousness. Do not feel ashamed to be nervous. There are famous actors who suffer terribly from nerves.

- Use a deep breathing technique to carry the word flow and calm the 'fight or flight' mode. (See Chapter Six, page 146.)

- Visualise the best possible speech scenario from the 'preparation' stage and keep believing that you are giving an excellent speech while delivering the presentation.

- Observe the audience neutrally, rather than looking inwards. (See Barbara Houseman's *Cameras out* technique in Chapter Six, page 158.)

- Maintain eye contact by focusing briefly on different members of the audience, without focusing for too long on any one individual. (See the section on *eye contact* in Chapter Six, page 153.)

- Pace the floor, if necessary, to reduce trembling caused by adrenaline flow.

- Never tell the audience you are nervous or unused to speaking. For some reason, audiences are not impressed by this!

- Try to smile.

- Great orators speak slowly. What sounds slow to the speaker should not be noticed by the audience, and allows them time to receive the message.

- Take questions only at the end of the presentation to avoid interruptions to flow during the presentation.

- If the answer to a question is not known, just say so.

Adrenalin

Adrenalin is useful and without adrenalin flow, delivery would be characterless. Breathing techniques are used to make the speaker appear outwardly calm at the beginning of the presentation, so that they are not physically shaking and have plenty of breath for the words to flow. Having achieved the physical and vocal appearance of calm at the beginning, the speaker should mentally calm down as the speech progresses.

Learning to drive

One of the key physical challenges for teenage and adult dyspraxics is learning to drive. Difficulties encountered in childhood when learning to ride a bicycle are re-visited, except this time, instead of having to learn to balance while holding onto and directing a handlebar and using two pedals, an adjustment has to be made between multiple gears and between three different pedals, while guiding a steering wheel!

For teenage and adult dyspraxics, driving can be very hard to achieve because of difficulties with:

- coordination
- spatial awareness
- sequencing
- concentration.

As a result of these difficulties, some dyspraxics may become demoralised and decide not to persevere with driving lessons and tests. Perhaps for some, driving is an impossible skill to master, but for others driving can be mastered with plenty of practice. (I should know, I took 11 driving tests!) The issue which is particularly concerning about the difficulties dyspraxics might face when driving, is that potential for careers and employability and essentially life fulfilment can so easily become less achievable without the use of a car.

Maxine Frances Roper discusses Laurence Roberts as an example of how difficult it can be for people with dyspraxia to learn to drive. The basics of driving had to be constantly reinforced and although he did a perfect reverse corner manoeuvre the first time, subsequently he could not reverse round a corner properly for several months. He tried to squeeze himself out of the door of the car during his first lesson, because it did not occur to him that he could open the door wider (*The Daily Telegraph* 2011).

For most dyspraxics, I would presume that learning to drive is difficult, and that even after the test has been passed, there can still be difficulties with spatial awareness and particular difficulties with parking manoeuvres. Certainly, in 2011, research found that fewer adults with DCD learn to drive than their non-DCD counterparts, and that those who do learn to drive report issues with calculation of distances and parking difficulties (Kirby, Sugden and Edwards 2011).

Strategies for driving

There are strategies which can be used to make driving easier:

- additional wing mirrors to assist with observation, parking and manoeuvring

- satellite navigation system for directions
- stickers as a reminder of 'left' and 'right'.

According to Mary Colley, a larger steering wheel, mounted high, can also be helpful to dyspraxic drivers (Colley 2006, p.74).

The Driver and Vehicle Standards Agency (DVSA) does offer adjustments for learner drivers with evidence of reading difficulties who are undertaking the driving theory test:

- test questions can be read by a voiceover
- extra time is available.

(Driver and Vehicle Standards Agency 2014)

The Forum of Mobility Centres can advise on physical adaptations which can be made to vehicles to assist with specific physical difficulties (www.mobility-centres.org.uk).

Driving proficiency

It should be noted that because people with dyspraxia are all individuals with different strengths and weaknesses, I have known dyspraxics who have passed their driving test first time and never fretted about how to drive or where to park. Some dyspraxics are naturally proficient drivers and it would be unfortunate to assume that just because a teenager has dyspraxia, driving will be difficult. Also, whatever difficulties are encountered in learning to drive, this does not mean that dyspraxics cannot become perfectly competent drivers. Like so many dyspraxic learning curves, driving may just take longer to achieve but, just like catching a ball or riding a bicycle, driving should improve coordination and spatial awareness.

CONCLUSION

Ultimately, whatever strengths are possessed by a dyspraxic individual, these cannot negate or compensate for the difficulties which accompany dyspraxia. Key difficulties faced by learners with dyspraxia are:

- Literacy, memory and physical difficulties, which can result in failure to reach full potential in the classroom and in exams.
- Physical difficulties with coordination and balance, joints and muscles.
- Embarrassing/humiliating experiences with clumsiness generally and in sports, causing low self-esteem.
- Difficulty with social skills, despite wanting to be sociable.
- Stress and anxiety resulting from dyspraxia.

Key strengths associated with dyspraxia are:

- Empathy for other people.
- Lateral thinking and problem-solving abilities.
- Having a perspective that deviates from the 'norm'.

Diagnosis

I belong to a generation where dyspraxia was scarcely heard of and it was unusual to be assessed for dyspraxia. Even now, there are a variety of assessments for children with DCD but there is no 'gold standard' means of assessment (Kirby and Sugden 2007b).

For the learner with dyspraxia, there is a real risk that their condition will remain unrecognised at home and in the classroom. This is why it is so important that dyspraxia is properly understood by teachers and by GPs who are responsible for making the referral for assessment. Does the complex nature of dyspraxia make initial screening difficult? Chartered psychologist David Grant believes that personal history is very important as an adjunct to psychological assessment and when assessors do not look at personal history, errors are made and, for example, dyspraxia can get overlooked in favour of dyslexia. For this reason, David Grant will:

> Ask questions about learning to drive, driving generally, work activities such as being employed in bars and cafes, and preparing food in the kitchen. Dyspraxia can affect the ability to judge distances and reverse park. It results in difficulties with carrying trays of drink and food. In the kitchen there is a tendency for dyspraxics to work slowly and carefully to avoid burns and cuts. (Grant n.d., p.9)

Dyspraxia has a silent voice: the secret dyspraxic. For every classroom learner who has been assessed as having dyspraxia, there will be learners with dyspraxic tendencies who will never be assessed or even realise that life is challenging because they have dyspraxia. Those learners with dyspraxic tendencies need the same support in the classroom and beyond as learners who have the 'label'.

Treatment

Are any of the other key SpLDs as complicated as dyspraxia? There remains a real lack of knowledge about dyspraxia and know-how can be limited even among those who can really help, for example teachers, GPs or occupational therapists. Tests for dyspraxia can be thorough or astonishingly minimal with, for example, the ability to throw a bean bag into a square being used as the sole measure of whether a child or adolescent might be dyspraxic or not. Each profession seems to have an awareness of different aspects of dyspraxia without necessarily having an understanding of the whole condition. Some children are referred to a psychologist for a dyspraxia assessment, while others are referred to an occupational therapist, but the perspective of these two professionals is different. Surely both the psychologist and the occupational therapist need to be involved for maximum benefit to be achieved for the child with dyspraxia? Educators also have a crucial role for dyspraxia, and recognising and accommodating it in the classroom, the seminar room or the lecture theatre can have a significant impact on the future success and well-being of the dyspraxic.

Research

Currently, research into dyslexia seems to be more prevalent than research into dyspraxia, possibly because dyspraxia is less well known. And yet this is a very exciting time for dyspraxia because of research into the significance of neurons. Over the next 20 years, there will be more neurological research into the brain and this should result in a greater understanding of dyspraxia.

The diversity of manifestations of dyspraxia is under-researched at the moment, and although Amanda Kirby has led research into some of the areas listed below, I would like to see more research on dyspraxia and associated difficulties, such as:

- birth difficulties
- the impact of the vestibular system on dyspraxia
- flat feet
- handedness
- eating – slowness and faddiness
- irritable bowel syndrome
- fibromyalgia
- joint problems, such as arthritis
- repetitive strain injury
- physical improvements achieved through practising sporting activities
- difficulties encountered in the classroom
- literacy
- driving
- remedial effect of strategies for supporting the dyspraxic mind
- working life experiences of dyspraxics.

Finally

Perhaps modern society is too keen to apply labels and there is a need to adjust to accommodate dyspraxia into society. Maybe expectations need to change. There needs to be more understanding of dyspraxia as a complex condition that has mental as well as physical consequences. There also needs to be greater awareness of the diversity of thinking skills that comes with dyspraxia, if learning is to accommodate the cognitive difficulties faced by the dyspraxic in any academic environment, at any age. The educational years are crucial for people with dyspraxia. If their needs are recognised and they are introduced to supportive strategies then, it is hoped, they will reach their full potential, live fulfilled lives and make a useful contribution to society, precisely because they are different.

REFERENCES

Arthritis Research UK (n.d.) *What causes work-related joint disorders?* Chesterfield: Arthritis Research UK. Accessed on 13/5/14 at www.arthritisresearchuk.org/arthritis-information/arthritis-and-daily-life/work-related-jd/what-causes-work-related-jd.aspx

Attwood, T. (2008) *The Complete Guide to Asperger's Syndrome.* London: Jessica Kingsley Publishers.

Aurelius, M. (2004) *Meditations.* London: Penguin. (Translated by Maxwell Staniforth).

Ayres, A.J. (1963) *The Development of Perceptual–Motor Abilities: A Theoretical Basis for Treatment of Dysfunction.* Eleanor Clarke Slagle Lecture. Bethesda: The American Occupational Therapy Association. Accessed on 17/6/14 at www.aota.org/-/media/Corporate/Files/Publications/AJOT/Slagle/1963.ashx

Bandler, R. and Grinder, J. (1979) *Frogs into Princes: The Introduction to Neuro-Linguistic Programming.* Moab, UT: Real People Press.

Barbe, W. and Swassing, R. (1979) *Teaching Through Modality Strengths: Concepts and Practices.* Columbus, OH: Zaner-Blosner.

Baron-Cohen, S., Bethlehem, R., Allison, C., Auyeung, B. *et al.* (2014) *Empathy in autism spectrum conditions.* Cambridge: Autism Research Centre (ARC), Cambridge University. Accessed on 31/7/14 at www.autismresearchcentre.com/project_1_empathy

Bath, J. and Knox, D. (1984) 'Two styles of performing mathematics.' In Bath, J., Chinn, S. and Knox, D. (eds) *Dyslexia: Research and its Applications to the Adolescent.* Bath: Better Books.

BBC (2010) *The Classroom Experiment.* BBC2, 27 September.

BBC Cymru (2003) '*The school gate for parents in Wales. Case study 1: Dyspraxia.*' Cardiff: BBC Cymru. Accessed on 6/6/14 at www.bbc.co.uk/wales/schoolgate/aboutschool/content/3specialneeds.shtml

Birnie, J. (n.d.) *Part B: Aspergers Syndrome: a difference rather than a 'mental health difficulty.* Gloucester: University of Gloucester. Accessed on 10/5/14 at www2.glos.ac.uk/gdn/icp/dasperg.pdf

Blowers, H. and Bryan, R. (2004) *Weaving a library Web: a guide to developing children's websites.* Chicago: American Library Association.

Boon, M. (2000) *Helping Children with Dyspraxia.* London: Jessica Kingsley Publishers.

Brennan, R. (1998) *The Alexander Technique: A Practical Introduction.* Shaftesbury: Element Books.

Bridgeman, E. and Snowling, M. (1988) 'The perception of phoneme sequence: a comparison of dyspraxic and normal children.' *International Journal of Language & Communication Disorders* 23, 3, December, 245–252. [online] London: Royal College of Speech and Language Therapists. Abstract accessed on 16/7/14 at http://onlinelibrary.wiley.com/doi/10.3109/13682828809011936/abstract

British Medical Journal (1962) '"Clumsy Children".' *British Medical Journal* 22 Dec, 2, 5320, 1665–1666.

Brontë, C. (1953) *Jane Eyre.* London: Collins. (Original work published 1847).

Brookes, G. (2007) *Dyspraxia.* 2nd ed. London: Continuum.

Burkeman, O. (2012) *The Antidote: Happiness for People Who Can't Stand Positive Thinking.* Edinburgh: Canongate.

Christmas, J. (2009) 'Demystifying Dyspraxia.' *Special Children Magazine* 190 August. London: Optimus Education. Accessed on 19/5/14 at http://specialchildren-magazine.com/feature/demystifying-dyspraxia

Colley, M. (2006) *Living with Dyspraxia.* Rev. ed. London: Jessica Kingsley Publishers.

Cooper, R. (n.d.) *Neurodiversity and Dyslexia: Compensatory strategies, or different approaches?* London: LSE. Accessed on 10/5/14 at brainhe.com/NeurodiversityandDyslexiabyRCooper.docx

Cowling, K. and H. (1993) *Toe by Toe: A Highly Structured Multi-sensory Reading Manual for Teachers and Parents.* Shipley: Toe by Toe.

Cuddy, A. (2012) *Your body language shapes who you are.* New York, NY: TED. Accessed on 1/7/14 at www.ted.com/talks/amy_cuddy_your_body_language_shapes_who_you_are

Daily Telegraph, The (2008a) 'Dyspraxia: clumsy but clever.' 19 April [online] London: Daily Telegraph. Accessed on 9/5/14 at www.telegraph.co.uk/health/3354324/Dyspraxia-clumsy-but-clever.html

Daily Telegraph, The (2008b) 'Harry Potter's Daniel Radcliffe has dyspraxia.' 17 August [online] London: Daily Telegraph. Accessed on 9/5/14 at www.telegraph.co.uk/news/celebritynews/2573230/Harry-Potters-Daniel-Radcliffe-has-dyspraxia.html

Daily Telegraph, The (2009a) 'Florence and the Machine interview: sound and vision.' 4 June [online] London: Daily Telegraph. Accessed on 9/5/14 at www.telegraph.co.uk/culture/music/rockandpopfeatures/5443013/Florence-and-the-Machine-interview-sound-and-vision.html

Daily Telegraph, The (2009b) 'Computer games good for children.' 21 December [online] London: Daily Telegraph. Accessed on 8/7/14 at www.telegraph.co.uk/science/science-news/6857907/Computer-games-good-for-children.html

Daily Telegraph, The (2011) 'Driving with dyspraxia.' 21 January [online] London: Daily Telegraph. Accessed on 13/6/14 at www.telegraph.co.uk/motoring/road-safety/8252720/Driving-with-dyspraxia.html

Decker, B. (2014) *Establishing Executive Presence.* 16 April [online blog] San Francisco: Decker Communications. Accessed on 1/7/14 http://decker.com/blog/tag/eye-contact/

Denckla, M. (1984) 'Developmental Dyspraxia: The Clumsy Child'. In: Levine, M and Satz, P. (eds.) (1984) *Middle Childhood: Development and Dysfunction.* Baltimore, MA: University Park Press.

Disability Salford (n.d.) The Gift of Dyspraxia. Salford: Disability Salford. Accessed on 11/11/14 at https://sites.google.com/site/disabilitysalford/home

Dixon, G and Addy, L. (2004) 'Handwriting and Dyspraxia'. Online extract from *Making Inclusion Work for Children with Dyspraxia: practical strategies for teachers.* London: Routledge. Accessed on 16/7/14 at www.dyspraxiainfo.co.uk/Handouts/Handwriting%20and%20Dyspraxia.%20%281%29.pdf

Dommett, E. (2011) 'Autism: a difference or disorder? Implications for access to services?' APPG on Scientific Research in Learning. *Science in Parliament* Spring 68, 1, 30. Accessed on 13/6/14 at www.futuremind.ox.ac.uk/downloads/Autism_SiP_article.pdf

Driver and Vehicle Standards Agency, The (2014) *The driving theory test for cars and motorcycles: if you have special needs.* London: Gov.Uk. Accessed on 13/6/14 at https://www.gov.uk/driving-theory-test/if-you-have-special-needs

Dyslexia Research Trust (n.d) *Vision & Coloured Filters.* Oxford: Dyslexia Research Trust. Accessed on 3/6/14 at www.dyslexic.org.uk/research/vision-coloured-filters

Dyspraxia Foundation (2012a) *Working with Dyspraxia: a hidden asset.* [Dyspraxia Foundation Guide for Employers] Cheltenham: Key 4 Learning. Accessed on 2/6/14 at www.dyspraxiafoundation.org.uk/downloads/dynamo_project/Employer_guide_to_dyspraxia_1.0.pdf

Dyspraxia Foundation (2012b) *Example Disclosure Document (Dynamo Project).* Hitchin: Dyspraxia Foundation. Accessed on 12/6/14 at www.dyspraxiafoundation.org.uk/downloads/dynamo_project/DF_Disclosure_Document_april_12.pdf

Dyspraxia Foundation (2013a) *Charity Challenges British Public About Attitudes Towards Dyspraxia.* Press Release. Hitchin: Dyspraxia Foundation. Accessed on 6/5/14 at www.dyspraxiafoundation.org.uk/charity-challenges-british-public-attitudes-dyspraxia/

Dyspraxia Foundation (2013b) *Seeing Your Way Through: Beat the Bullies – A Guide for Children.* Hitchin: Dyspraxia Foundation. Accessed on 26/6/14 at www.dyspraxiafoundation.org.uk/wp-content/uploads/2013/10/Bully_kids.pdf

Dyspraxia Foundation (2013c) *Seeing Your Way Through: Bullying – A Guide for Parents.* Hitchin: Dyspraxia Foundation. Accessed on 26/6/14 at www.dyspraxiafoundation.org.uk/wp-content/uploads/2013/10/Bully_parents.pdf

Dyspraxia Foundation (2014a) *Dyspraxia in adulthood.* Hitchin: Dyspraxia Foundation. Accessed on 6/5/14 at www.dyspraxiafoundation.org.uk/dyspraxia-adults/living-dyspraxia/

Dyspraxia Foundation (2014b) *Dyspraxia at a glance.* Hitchin: Dyspraxia Foundation. Accessed on 13/8/14 at www.dyspraxiafoundation.org.uk/about-dyspraxia/dyspraxia-glance/

Dyspraxia Foundation (2014c) *So what is going on in the brain?* Hitchin: Dyspraxia Foundation. Accessed on 6/5/14 at www.dyspraxiafoundation.org.uk/about-dyspraxia/brain/

Dyspraxia Foundation (2014d) *About dyspraxia: FAQs.* Hitchin: Dyspraxia Foundation. Accessed on 8/7/14 at www.dyspraxiafoundation.org.uk/faqs/

Dyspraxia Foundation (2014e) *Reading and spelling.* Hitchin: Dyspraxia Foundation. Accessed on 16/7/14 at www.dyspraxiafoundation.org.uk/about-dyspraxia/reading-spelling/

Dyspraxia Foundation (2014f) *Dyspraxia in Adults – Symptoms.* Hitchin: Dyspraxia Foundation. Accessed on 6/5/14 at www.dyspraxiafoundation.org.uk/services/ad_symptoms.php

Dyspraxia Support Group of New Zealand, The (n.d.) *What is dyspraxia?* Christchurch, NZ: The Dyspraxia Support Group of New Zealand. Accessed on 28/5/14 at www.dyspraxia.org.nz/index.php?page=what-is-dyspraxia

Dzuik, M., Gidley Larson, J., Apostu, A., Mahone, E., Denckla, M. and Mostofsky, S. (2007) 'Dyspraxia in autism: association with motor, social, and communicative deficits.' *Developmental Medicine and Child Neurology* 49, 10, 734–739. London: Wiley.

Economic and Social Research Council (ESRC) (2006) *Leeds Consensus Statement. Development Coordination Disorder as a Specific Learning Difficulty.* Consensus Meeting Series 2004–2006. [Principal Investigating Professor: Sugden, D.] Leeds University: ESRC. Accessed on 8/5/14 at www.dcd-uk.org/images/LeedsConsensus06.pdf.

Edwards, J., Berube, M., Erlandson, K., Haug, S. *et al.* (2011) 'Developmental coordination disorder in school-aged children born very preterm and/or at very low birth weight: a systematic review.' *Journal of Developmental & Behavioral Pediatrics* Nov, 32, 9, 678–'87. [online] McLean, VA: Society for Developmental and Behavioral Pediatrics. Abstract accessed on 7/7/14 at www.ncbi.nlm.nih.gov/pubmed/21900828.

Epictetus (2014) *The Enchiridion.* (Translated by Thomas Higginson.) Salt Lake City: Project Gutenberg Literary Archive Foundation. Accessed on 24/6/14 at www.gutenberg.org/files/45109/45109-h/45109-h.htm (Original work spoken between 55 and 135AD.)

Equality and Human Rights Commission (2009) *GCHQ: Embracing neurodiversity and the benefits for the business. [Extract from an unpublished Commission report A Model for Employment Valuing Neurodiversity]* Accessed on 16/6/14 at www.equalityhumanrights.com/advice-and-guidance/working-better/disability-report/case-studies/gchq/

Food and Behaviour Research (2003) *Factsheet: Fatty Acids in Dyslexia, Dyspraxia, ADHD and the Autistic Spectrum – An Overview.* Oxford: Food and Behaviour Research, Mansfield College. Accessed on 19/5/14 at www.fabresearch.org/viewItem.php?id=6702&listId=1401&categoryId=&navPageId=1400

Gathercole, S. and Packiam Alloway, T. (2007) *Understanding Working Memory: A Classroom Guide.* London: Harcourt Assessment. Accessed on 10/6/14 at www.york.ac.uk/res/wml/Classroom%20guide.pdf

Gibbs, J., Appleton, J. and Appleton, R. (2007) 'Dyspraxia or developmental coordination disorder? Unravelling the enigma.' *Archives of Disease in Childhood* 92, 6, 534–539. [online] London: British Medical Association. Accessed on 8/5/14 at www.ncbi.nlm.nih.gov/pmc/articles/PMC2066137/

Gov.Uk. (2014) Access to Work. London: Gov.Uk. Accessed on 13/11/14 at https://www.gov.uk/access-to-work/what-youll-get

Grant, D. (n.d.) *Formal identification of a range of specific learning differences.* London: LSE. Accessed on 9/6/14 at brainhe.com/resources/documents/DGrantsep.doc

Graybiel, A. and Rauch S. (2000) 'Toward a Neurobiology Review of Obsessive-Compulsive Disorder.' *Neuron* 28, 343–347. Cambridge, MA: Cell Press. http://web.mit.edu/bcs/graybiel-lab/publications/Neuron_Graybiel.pdf

Guardian, The (1985) 'Don't look now, but no one's looking.' 11 June. London: Guardian.

Guardian, The (2005) 'Something happened…' 21 May [online] London: Guardian. Accessed on 26/6/14 at www.guardian.co.uk/books/2005/may/21/fiction.features/print

Guardian, The (2010) 'A bunch of dead muscles, thinking.' 9 January [online] London: Guardian. Accessed on 10/6/14 at www.theguardian.com/theguardian/2010/jan/09/tony-judt-motor-neurone-disease

Guardian, The (2011a) 'What I'm really thinking: The person with Asperger's syndrome.' 15 January [online] Accessed on 1/7/14 at www.theguardian.com/lifeandstyle/2011/jan/15/really-thinking-aspergers-person

Guardian, The (2011b) 'An afternoon nap is good for your health.' 2 March [online] London: Guardian. Accessed on 25/6/14 at www.guardian.co.uk/lifeandstyle/2011/mar/02/afternoon-nap-good-for-you)

Guardian, The (2013a) '5:2 your life – the worry diet.' 15 June [online] London: Guardian. Accessed on 28/6/14 at www.theguardian.com/lifeandstyle/2013/jun/15/5-2-your-life-worry-jon-ronson

Guardian, The (2013b) 'Former death row couple: 'Life turned out beautifully'.' 22 June [online] London: Guardian. Accessed on 28/6/14 at www.theguardian.com/lifeandstyle/2013/jun/22/former-death-row-couple

Hakim, A.J. (2013) *Hypermobility & Illness*. Plymouth: Hypermobility Syndromes Association. Accessed on 13/5/14 at http://hypermobility.org/help-advice/hypermobility-syndromes/what-is-hms/

Hall, D. (1988) 'Clumsy children.' *British Medical Journal* 296, 6619, 375–376. [online] London: British Medical Journal. Accessed on 16/5/14 at www.ncbi.nlm.nih.gov/pmc/articles/PMC2544964/pdf/bmj00271-0003.pdf

Hanes, D. and McCollum, G. (2006) 'Cognitive-vestibular interactions: A review of patient difficulties and possible mechanisms.' *Journal of Vestibular Research* 16, 75–91. [online] Amsterdam: IOS Press. Accessed on 28/5/14 at www.clas.ufl.edu/users/msscha/CSDCSS/vestibular_cogdeficit.pdf

Harrison, E. (n.d.) *Mindfulness or Meditation?* Perth: Perth Meditation Centre. Accessed on 30/6/14 at www.perthmeditationcentre.com.au/articles/mindfulness-or-meditation.htm

Harvard Medical School (2013) *Regular exercise releases brain chemicals key for memory, concentration, and mental sharpness*. Boston: Harvard Health Publications. Accessed on 11/6/14 at www.health.harvard.edu/press_releases/regular-exercise-releases-brain-chemicals-key-for-memory-concentration-and-mental-sharpness

Hegarty, S. (2012) 'The myth of the eight-hour sleep.' *BBC News Magazine* 22 Feb. [online] London: BBC. Accessed on 24/6/14 at www.bbc.co.uk/news/magazine-16964783

Hirschberg, L. (2013) *Do you have your thoughts, or do your thoughts have you?* Cambridge, MA: Neurodevelopment Center. Accessed on 24/6/14 at http://neurodevelopmentcenter.com/do-your-thoughts-have-you/

Holder, M. (2005a) *Public Interest Survey*. Bloomington: Handedness Research Institute, CISAB. Accessed on 21/5/14 at www.indiana.edu/~primate/forms/hand.html

Holder, M. (2005b) *What does Handedness have to do with Brain Lateralization (and who cares?)?* Bloomington: Handedness Research Institute, CISAB. Accessed on 10/7/14 at www.indiana.edu/~primate/brain.html

Holsti, L., Grunau, R. and Whitfield, M. (2002) 'Developmental coordination disorder in extremely low birth weight children at nine years.' *Journal of Developmental & Behavioral Pediatrics* February, 23, 1, 9–15. [online] McLean, VA: Society for Developmental and Behavioral Pediatrics. Abstract accessed on 7/7/14 at www.ncbi.nlm.nih.gov/pubmed/11889346.

Hopscotch Children's Therapy Centre (2012) *Theory of Sensory Integration*. London: Hopscotch Children's Therapy Centre. Accessed on 17/6/14 at www.hopscotchtherapy.co.uk/sensoryintegration.html

Hornsby, B., Shear, F. and Pool, J. (2006) *Alpha to Omega: the A–Z of teaching reading, writing and spelling*. Portsmouth: Heinemann.

Houseman, B. (2008) *Tackling Text [And Subtext]: A Step-by-Step Guide for Actors*. London: Nick Hern.

Jensen, E. (2000) 'Moving with the Brain in Mind'. *Educational Leadership* November, 34–37. Alexandria, VA: ASCD.

Kabat-Zinn, Jon. (2004) *Wherever You Go, There You Are: Mindfulness meditation for everyday life.* London: Piatkus.

Kates, C. (n.d.) *Orthotic Treatment of Flat Feet in Children with Low Muscle Tone.* Seattle: Boyer Children's Clinic. Accessed on 18/5/14 at www.boyercc.org/media/7662/ebp_orthotic_treatment.doc

Khoury, B., Lecomte, T., Fortin, G., Masse, M. *et al. (2013)* 'Mindfulness-based therapy: a comprehensive meta-analysis.' *Clinical Psychology Review* August, 33, 6, 763–71. [online] Philadelphia, PA: Elsevier. Abstract accessed on 30/6/14 at www.ncbi.nlm.nih.gov/pubmed/23796855

Kirby, A. (1999) *Dyspraxia: the hidden handicap.* London: Souvenir.

Kirby, A., Davies, R. and Bryant, A. (2005) 'Do teachers know more about specific learning difficulties than general practitioners' British Journal of Special Education 32, 3, 122–126. London: Wiley.

Kirby, A. and Davies, R. (2007a) 'Developmental Coordination Disorder and Joint Hypermobility Syndrome--overlapping disorders? Implications for research and clinical practice.' *Child: Care, Health and Development* 33, 5, 513–519. [online] London: Wiley. Abstract accessed on 18/5/14 at www.ncbi.nlm.nih.gov/pubmed/17725772

Kirby, A and Sugden, D. (2007b) 'Children with developmental coordination disorders.' *Journal of the Royal Society of Medicine* April, 100, 4, 182–186. [online] London: Royal Society of Medicine. Accessed on 6/5/14 at www.ncbi.nlm.nih.gov/pmc/articles/PMC1847727/

Kirby, A., Sugden, D. and Edwards, L. (2011) 'Driving Behaviour in Young Adults with Developmental Co-ordination Disorder.' *Journal of Adult Development,* 18, 3, 122–129. [online] Heidelberg: Springer. Abstract accessed on 16/6/14 at http://link.springer.com/article/10.1007%2 Fs10804-011-9120-4

Knight, S. (2010) *NLP at Work.* Yarmouth, ME: Nicholas Brealey Publishing.

Kurtz, L. (2007) *Understanding Motor Skills in Children with Dyspraxia, ADHD, Autism, and Other Learning Disabilities: A Guide to Improving Coordination.* London: Jessica Kingsley Publishers.

Laboratory of Vestibular Neurophysiology (n.d.) The *Research and Clinical Trials: Laboratory of Vestibular Neurophysiology.* Baltimore: Johns Hopkins Outpatient Center. Accessed on 18/5/14 at www. hopkinsmedicine.org/otolaryngology/research/vestibular/

Ladybird Books (2014) *Key Words.* London: Ladybird Books. Accessed on 17/6/14 at www.ladybird. com/ageandstage/school/key_words.html

Laidler, G. (1942) *Pont.* London: Collins.

Leahy, R. (2005) *The Worry Cure.* [Kindle] London: Hachette Digital.

Lee, M. and Smith, G. (1998) 'The Effectiveness of Physiotherapy for Dyspraxia.' *Physiotherapy* 84, 6, 276–284.

Lienhard, J. (n.d.) *'Ricci's Memory Palace.'* Engines of Our Ingenuity. Houston Public Radio, Episode 1226. Houston: College of Engineering, University of Houston. Accessed on 10/6/14 at www.uh.edu/engines/epi1226.htm

Listen and Learn Centre (2011) *Dyspraxia – a motor planning disorder.* Victoria: Listen and Learn Centre. Accessed on 10/5/14 at www.listenandlearn.com.au/disorders_dyspraxia.asp

Lobban, I. (2012) *GCHQ and Turing's Legacy.* Speech delivered at University of Leeds on 4 October 2012. Cheltenham: GCHQ. Accessed on 16/6/14 at www.gchq.gov.uk/press_and_media/ speeches/Pages/speech-in-tribute-to-Alan-Turing.aspx

Lucker, J. (2012) *What is it like to have an auditory processing disorder?* Washington DC: National Coalition of Auditory Processing Disorders (NCAPD). Accessed on 1/6/14 at www.ncapd. org/uploads/APD_simulation_aug_2012.pdf

Lyons, C., Payton, P. and Winfield, M. (1999) 'A study of the possible benefits of the Alexander Technique for children exhibiting comorbidity of dyslexia and dyspraxia.' *Dyslexia Review* 11, 2, 18–20.

Marash, J. (1947) *Effective Speaking: A Course in Elocution.* London: Harrap & Co.

McCleery, J, Elliott, N., Sampanis, D. and Stefanidou, C. (2013) 'Motor development and motor resonance difficulties in autism: relevance to early intervention for language and communication skills.' *Frontiers in Integrative Neuroscience* 7 [online] Lausanne: Frontiers. Accessed on 8/5/14 at www.ncbi.nlm.nih.gov/pmc/articles/PMC3634796/

McGonigal. K. (2009) 'Change Your Posture: Change your mind and mood.' *Psychology Today,* 5 Oct. [online book extract] New York: Psychology Today. Accessed on 26/6/14 at www. psychologytoday.com/blog/the-science-willpower/200910/change-your-posture

McMurray, S. (n.d.) *Resource File for Special Educational Needs: Understanding Memory Difficulties*. Bangor: Department of Education Northern Ireland. Accessed on 10/6/14 at www.deni.gov.uk/06_understanding_memory.pdf

Medical News Today (2007) 'Novel Study Sheds Light on Imitation Learning.' *Medical News Today* 21 March. Bexhill on Sea: MNT. Accessed on 16/5/14 at www.medicalnewstoday.com/releases/65591.php

Moller, R. (n.d.) *The Scottish Dyspraxion* (blog). [currently offline] Accessed on 6/5/12 at http://ndscotland.blogspot.co.uk/p/work_05.html

Morley, M. (2006) *Aching Back? Sitting Up Straight Could Be the Culprit*. RSNA Press Release, 27 November. Chicago, IL: Radiological Society of North America. Accessed on 3/6/14 at http://www2.rsna.org/timssnet/media/pressreleases/pr_target.cfm?ID=294

Morrison, S., Ferrari, J. and Smillie, S. (2013) 'Assessment of gait characteristics and orthotic management in children with Developmental Coordination Disorder: Preliminary findings to inform multidisciplinary care.' *Research in Developmental Disabilities* 34, 10, 3197–3201. [online] Philadelphia: Elsevier. Abstract accessed on 8/7/14 at www.sciencedirect.com/science/article/pii/S0891422213002618

Nagamatsu, L., Chan, A., Davis, C. and Beattie, B. (2013) 'Physical Activity Improves Verbal and Spatial Memory in Older Adults with Probable Mild Cognitive Impairment: A 6-Month Randomized Controlled Trial.' *Journal of Aging Research* 861893. [online] New York, NY: Hindawi Publishing Corporation. Accessed on 10/6/14 at www.ncbi.nlm.nih.gov/pmc/articles/PMC3595715/

National Autistic Society. (2014) *Dyspraxia and autism spectrum disorders*. London: The National Autistic Society. Accessed on 9/5/14 at www.autism.org.uk/about-autism/related-conditions/dyspraxia/dyspraxia-and-autism-spectrum-disorders.aspx

National Institute of Health and National Institute of Neurological Disorders and Stroke (2005) *The Brain: Our Sense of Self. Teacher's Guide: Information about the Brain*. Bethesda: NIH/NINDS. Accessed on 13/7/14 at http://science.education.nih.gov/supplements/nih4/self/guide/info-brain.htm

National Sleep Foundation (2013) *How Much Sleep Do We Really Need?* Arlington, VA: National Sleep Foundation. Accessed on 25/6/14 at www.sleepfoundation.org/article/how-sleep-works/how-much-sleep-do-we-really-need

Nichols, R. (1980) *The Struggle to be Human*. ILA Convention, Atlanta. Belle Pleine, MN: International Listening Association. Accessed on 2/7/14 at Atlanwww.listen.org/Resources/Documents/14.pdf

Oxford Dictionaries (2014) *Common misspellings*. Oxford: Oxford University Press. Accessed on 4/6/14 at www.oxforddictionaries.com/words/common-misspellings

Paulos, E and Goodman, E. (2004) *The Familiar Stranger: Anxiety, Comfort, and Play in Public Place*. Pittsburgh: Carnegie Mellon University. Accessed on 2/7/14 at http://repository.cmu.edu/cgi/viewcontent.cgi?article=1213&context=hcii

Pollock, N. (2009) 'Sensory integration: a review of the current state of the evidence.' *Occupational Therapy Now* 11.5, 6–10. Ottawa: Canadian Association of Occupational Therapists. Accessed on 2/7/14 at www.canchild.ca/en/canchildresources/resources/Sensory%20Integration.pdf

Praag, H. van, Kempermann, G. and Gage, F. (1999) 'Running increases cell proliferation and neurogenesis in the adult mouse dentate gyrus.' *Nature Neuroscience* 2, 266 – 270. [online] New York: Nature Neuroscience. Accessed on 11/6/14 at www.nature.com/neuro/journal/v2/n3/full/nn0399_266.html

Pratt, M. and Hill, E. (2010) *Anxiety and behavioural difficulties in children diagnosed with DCD*. Developmental Coordination Disorder Research UK Conference. York St. John University, 8 July 2010. London: UCL. Accessed on 27/6/14 at www.yorksj.ac.uk/pdf/Anxiety%20and%20Behavioural%20difficulties%20in%20children%20diagnosed%20with%20DCD%20M%20Pratt%20and%20E%20Hill.pdf

Quast, L. (2013) *5 Tips To Create A Positive First Impression*. [online] New York, NY: Forbes.com. Accessed on 9/11/14 at www.forbes.com/sites/lisaquast/2013/09/09/5-tips-to-create-a-positive-first-impression/

Rawlinson, G. (1999) 'Reibadailty.' *New Scientist*, 162, 2188, 55. Sutton: Reed Business Information. Accessed on 3/6/14 at www.mrc-cbu.cam.ac.uk/people/matt.davis/Cmabrigde/newscientist_letter/

Revised English Bible, The (1989) *Proverbs.* 15 v.1. Oxford: OUP, Cambridge: CUP.

Rosner, J. and Simon, D. (1970) *The auditory analysis test: an initial report.* Pittsburgh: Pittsburgh University. Accessed on 4/6/14 at http://files.eric.ed.gov/fulltext/ED051253.pdf

Rowh, M. (2012) 'First Impressions Count.' *gradPSYCH Magazine*, Nov, 32. [online] Washington DC: American Psychological Association. Accessed on 26/6/14 at www.apa.org/gradpsych/2012/11/first-impressions.aspx

Sackville Stoner, W. (1919) *The History of the United States.* [poem – original publication details unknown]

Sayler, S. (2010) *What Your Body Says (And How to Master the Message): Inspire, Influence, Build Trust and Create Lasting Business Relationships.* [Kindle] Hoboken, NJ: John Wiley & Sons.

Sadock, B. and Sadock, V. (2009) *Kaplan and Sadock's Concise Textbook of Child and Adolescent Psychiatry.* 10th ed. Philadelphia, PA: Lippincott, Williams & Wilkins.

Shattock, P and Whiteley, P. (2004) 'Biomedical Approaches to Dyspraxia and Related Disorders.' *Dyspraxia Foundation Professional Journal* 2004 3, 6–15. [online] Hitchin: Dyspraxia Foundation. Accessed on 18/5/14 at www.dyspraxiafoundation.org.uk/downloads/Professional_Journal_Issue_3.pdf

Sillito, D. (2011) *Is 'happiness' a skill you can learn?* London: BBC Breakfast. Accessed on 30/6/14 at www.bbc.co.uk/news/12263893

Sillito, D. (2012) *Mind over matter: Can meditation bring happiness?* London: BBC Breakfast. Accessed on 30/6/14 at www.bbc.co.uk/news/health-16389183

Skill: National Bureau for Students with Disabilities (2005) *Telling people about your disability.* Accessed on 12/6/14 at www.skill.org.uk/uploads/Tellingpeople.doc

Skinner, R. and Piek, J. (2001) 'Psychosocial implications of poor motor coordination in children and adolescents.' *Human Movement Science* Mar, 20, 1–2, 73–94. [online] Philadelphia, PA: Elsevier. Abstract accessed on 24/6/14 at www.ncbi.nlm.nih.gov/pubmed/11471399

Solan, H., Shelley-Tremblay, J. and Larson, S. (2007) 'Vestibular Function, Sensory Integration, and Balance Anomalies: A Brief Literature Review.' *Optometry and Vision Development* 38, 1, 13–17. [online] Aurora, OH: College of Optometrists in Vision Development. Accessed on 16/7/14 at http://c.ymcdn.com/sites/www.covd.org/resource/resmgr/ovd38-1/13-18solan.pdf

SpLD Assessment Standards Committee (SASC) (2013) *Updated guidance on the assessment of DCD/dyspraxia.* Evesham: SASC/STEC. Accessed on 10/7/14 at *www.sasc.org.uk/SASCDocuments/Dyspraxia%20guidance%20SASC-STEC%20Sept%202013.pdf*

Steinman, K., Mostofsky, S. and Denckla, M. (2010) 'Toward a Narrower, More Pragmatic View of Developmental Dyspraxia'. *Journal of Child Neurology* January, 25, 1, 71–81. Thousand Oaks, CA: Sage Publications. Accessed on 25/6/14 at www.ncbi.nlm.nih.gov/pmc/articles/PMC2892896/pdf/nihms193792.pdf

Stock Kranowitz, C. (2005) *The Out-Of-Sync Child: Recognizing and Coping with Sensory Processing Disorder.* New York, NY: Penguin.

Sutton Hamilton, S. (2002) 'Evaluation of Clumsiness in Children.' *American Family Physician* 66, 8, October 15, 1435–1441. [online] Leawood, Kansas: American Academy of Family Physicians. Accessed on 9/11/14 at www.aafp.org/afp/2002/1015/p1435.html

Times Educational Supplement, The (2003) 'Dyspraxia.' 17 October [online] London: TES. Accessed on 10/5/14 at www.tes.co.uk/article.aspx?storycode=385417

Todd, J. (2011) *'Reframe thinking from disability to different ability'.* The Dyslexia and Dyspraxia Toolkit: Enabling a Whole Organisation Approach. London: Civil Service. Accessed on 10/5/14 at www.civilservice.gov.uk/wp-content/uploads/2011/09/appraisal_tcm6-6228.pdf

Tolle, E. (2005) *The Power of Now.* London: Hodder and Stoughton.

Tolle, E. (2009) *A New Earth.* London: Penguin.

Tyler, A. (1992) *Searching for Caleb.* London: Vintage.

UNESCO (2004) *The Plurality of Literacy and its Implications for Policies and Programmes.* Paris: UNESCO. Accessed on 2/6/14 at http://unesdoc.unesco.org/images/0013/001362/136246e.pdf

University of East London (n.d.) *Dyspraxia.* London: UEL. Accessed on 6/5/14 at www.uel.ac.uk/studentservices/supportingyou/staff/dyspraxia.htm

University of Hull (n.d(a)) *Understanding Dyslexia and Dyspraxia.* Hull: University of Hull. Accessed on 6/5/14 at http://www2.hull.ac.uk/student/pdf/dyswhatunderstanding.pdf

University of Hull (n.d(b)) *Understanding your own intelligence strengths.* Hull: University of Hull. Accessed on 21/5/14 at http://www2.hull.ac.uk/student/pdf/dysbrainmultiple.pdf

Vandever, K. (2014) *The Eyes Have IT: The Importance of Making Eye Contact for IT Professionals.* Atlanta, GA: Association of Information Technology Professionals. Accessed on 1/7/14 at www.aitpatlanta.org/index.php?option=com_content&view=article&id=279:the-eyes-have-it-the-importance-of-making-eye-contact-for-it-professionals&catid=23:business&Itemid=187

Versfeld, P. (2007) *Developmental coordination disorder and dyspraxia.* Cape Town: Skills for Action. Accessed on 6/5/14 at www.skillsforaction.com/node/16

Vestibular Disorders Association. (2014a) *Types of vestibular disorders.* Portland, OR: Vestibular Disorders Association. Accessed on 15/5/14 at http://vestibular.org/understanding-vestibular-disorder/types-vestibular-disorders

Vestibular Disorders Association. (2014b) *The Human Balance System.* Portland, OR: Vestibular Disorders Association. Accessed on 15/5/14 at http://vestibular.org/understanding-vestibular-disorder/human-balance-system

Walker, M. (1992) *A Resource Pack for Tutors of Students with Specific Learning Difficulties.* Solihull: Marion Walker.

Werner, J., Cermak, S. and Aziz-Zadeh, L. (2012) 'Neural Correlates of Developmental Coordination Disorder: The Mirror Neuron System Hypothesis.' *Journal of Behavioral and Brain Science* 2, 258–268. [online] Delaware: SCIRP. Accessed on 18/5/14 at http://dx.doi.org/10.4236/jbbs.2012.22029

West, T. (1991) *The Mind's Eye: Visual Thinkers, Gifted People with Learning Difficulties, Computer Imaging, and the Ironies of Creativity.* London: Prometheus Books UK.

Williams, C. (2013) 'DCD/Dyspraxia in Primary School: An OT Perspective.' *Patoss Bulletin* 26, 1, 36–39. Evesham: Patoss.

Williams, M. (2014) *3-minute breathing space.* Oxford: Oxford Mindfulness Centre. Accessed on 30/6/14 at http://oxfordmindfulness.org/learn/resources/#brspace

Williams, M. and Penman, D. (2011) *Mindfulness: A practical guide to finding peace in a frantic world.* London: Piatkus.

Williams, Dr S. (n.d.) 'Listening Effectively.' *Leader Letter.* Dayton, Ohio: Wright State University. Accessed on 11.8.14 at www.wright.edu/~scott.williams/skills/listening.htm

Yahoo! Answers (2007) *Why do people ignore each other?* California: Yahoo. Accessed on 2/7/14 at https://answers.yahoo.com/question/index?qid=20071216195258AALZrXL

Yukelson, D. (n.d.) *Teaching Athletes Visualization and Mental Imagery Skills.* Pennsylvania: Penn State University. Accessed on 26/6/14 at www.mascsa.psu.edu/dave/Visualization-Handout.pdf

Zwicker, J., Yoon, S., Mackay, M., Petrie-Thomas, J., Rogers, M. and Synnes, A. (2013) 'Perinatal and neonatal predictors of developmental coordination disorder in very low birthweight children.' *Archives of Disease in Childhood* February, 98, 2, 118–122. [online] London: British Medical Association. Abstract accessed on 7/7/14 at www.ncbi.nlm.nih.gov/pubmed/23264434

SUBJECT INDEX

AUTHOR INDEX